my **revis** ...tes

AS Edexcel History
BRITISH POLITICAL
HISTORY, 1945–90
CONSENSUS AND CONFLICT

Robin Bunce
Laura Gallagher

HODDER
EDUCATION
AN HACHETTE UK COMPANY

The Publishers would like to thank the following for permission to reproduce copyright material:

Photo credits p.21 © Mirrorpix.

Note: The wording and structure of some written sources have been adapted and simplified to make them accessible to all students, while faithfully preserving the sense of the original.

Hachette UK's policy is to use papers that are natural, renewable and recyclable products and made from wood grown in sustainable forests. The logging and manufacturing processes are expected to conform to the environmental regulations of the country of origin.

Orders: please contact Bookpoint Ltd, 130 Milton Park, Abingdon, Oxon OX14 4SB.
Telephone: +44 (0)1235 827720. Fax: +44 (0)1235 400454. Lines are open 9.00a.m.–5.00p.m., Monday to Saturday, with a 24-hour message answering service. Visit our website at www.hoddereducation.co.uk

© Robin Bunce and Laura Gallagher 2014
First published in 2014 by
Hodder Education,
An Hachette UK Company
338 Euston Road
London NW1 3BH

Impression number 10 9 8 7 6 5 4 3 2
Year   2018 2017 2016 2015 2014

Cover photo © razihusin – Fotolia
Illustrations by Datapage (India) Pvt. Ltd
Typeset in 11/13 Stempel Schneidler Std by Datapage (India) Pvt. Ltd
Printed in India
A catalogue record for this title is available from the British Library
ISBN 978 1444 199536

Contents

Introduction

About Unit 2

Unit 2 is worth 50 per cent of your AS level. It requires detailed knowledge of a period of British history and the ability to explore and analyse historical sources. Overall, 60 per cent of the marks available are awarded for source analysis (Assessment Objective 2) and 40 per cent for using own knowledge to form an explanation (Assessment Objective 1).

In the exam, you are required to answer one question with two parts. Part (a) is worth 20 marks and Part (b) is worth 40 marks. It is advisable to spend approximately one-third of your time in the exam on Part (a) and the remaining two-thirds on Part (b). There will be a choice of two Part (b) questions, of which you must answer one.

Part (a) focuses on AO1. It will test your ability to:

■ comprehend source material
■ compare source material in detail, explaining how the sources agree and differ
■ suggest reasons why the sources agree or differ based on their provenance
■ reach an overall judgement.

Part (b) focuses on both AO1 and AO2. It will test your ability to:

■ select information that focuses on the question
■ organise this information to provide an answer to the question
■ integrate information from the sources and your own knowledge
■ weigh evidence from sources and your own knowledge to reach an overall judgement.

British Political History, 1945–90: Consensus and Conflict

The exam board specifies that students should study four general areas as part of this topic.

1. The Labour Governments of 1945–1951: reasons for the Labour election victory in 1945, domestic policies and how far this period was an 'age of austerity'.

2. The Conservative Governments of 1951–1964: the extent of consensus with Labour, domestic policies and changes in living standards.

3. Labour and Conservative Governments between 1964 and 1979: the nature and causes of domestic problems

4. The Conservative Governments of 1979–1990: reasons for the Conservative election victory of 1979, domestic policies, controversies and the reasons for the fall of Thatcher in 1990.

How to use this book

This book has been designed to help you to develop the knowledge and skills necessary to succeed in this exam. The book is divided into four sections – one for each general area of the course. Each section is made up of a series of topics organised into double-page spreads. On the left-hand page, you will find a summary of the key content you need to learn. Words in bold in the key content are defined in the glossary (see pages 73–74). On the right-hand page, you will find exam-focused activities. Together, these two strands of the book will take you through the knowledge and skills essential for exam success.

▼ Key historical content   ▼ Exam-focused activities

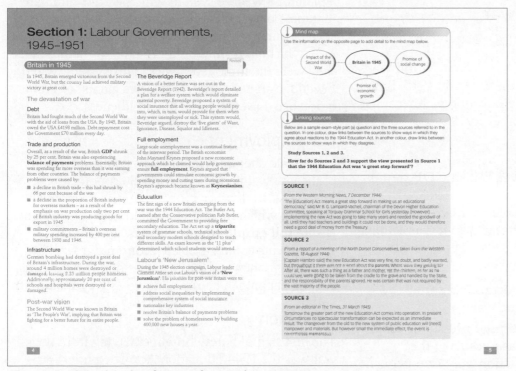

There are three levels of exam-focused activities.

- Band 1 activities are designed to develop the foundational skills needed to pass the exam. These have a turquoise heading and this symbol:

- Band 2 activities are designed to build on the skills developed in Band 1 activities and to help you achieve a C grade. These have an orange heading and this symbol:

- Band 3 activities are designed to enable you to access the highest grades. These have a purple heading and this symbol:

Some activities have answers or suggested answers on pages 75–77 and have the following symbol to indicate this:

Each section ends with an exam-style question and model A-grade answer with examiner's commentary. This should give you guidance on what is required to achieve the top grades. You can see the mark scheme on page 78.

You can also keep track of your revision by ticking off each topic heading in the book or by ticking the checklist on the contents page. Tick each box when you have:

- revised and understood a topic
- completed the activities.

Section 1: Labour Governments, 1945–1951

In 1945, Britain emerged victorious from the Second World War, but the country had achieved military victory at great cost.

The devastation of war

Debt

Britain had fought much of the Second World War with the aid of loans from the USA. By 1945, Britain owed the USA £4198 million. Debt repayment cost the Government £70 million every day.

Trade and production

Overall, as a result of the war, British **GDP** shrunk by 25 per cent. Britain was also experiencing **balance of payments** problems. Essentially, Britain was spending far more overseas than it was earning from other countries. The balance of payments problems were caused by:

- a decline in British trade – this had shrunk by 66 per cent because of the war
- a decline in the proportion of British industry for overseas markets – as a result of the emphasis on war production only two per cent of British industry was producing goods for export in 1945
- military commitments – Britain's overseas military spending increased by 400 per cent between 1938 and 1946.

Infrastructure

German bombing had destroyed a great deal of Britain's infrastructure. During the war, around 4 million homes were destroyed or damaged, leaving 2.25 million people homeless. Additionally, approximately 20 per cent of schools and hospitals were destroyed or damaged.

Post-war vision

The Second World War was known in Britain as 'The People's War', implying that Britain was fighting for a better future for its entire people.

The Beveridge Report

A vision of a better future was set out in the Beveridge Report (1942). Beveridge's report detailed a plan for a welfare system which would eliminate material poverty. Beveridge proposed a system of social insurance that all working people would pay into, which, in turn, would provide for them when they were unemployed or sick. This system would, Beveridge argued, destroy the 'five giants' of Want, Ignorance, Disease, Squalor and Idleness.

Full employment

Large-scale unemployment was a continual feature of the interwar period. The British economist John Maynard Keynes proposed a new economic approach which he claimed would help governments ensure **full employment**. Keynes argued that governments could stimulate economic growth by spending money and cutting taxes during recessions. Keynes's approach became known as **Keynesianism**.

Education

The first sign of a new Britain emerging from the war was the 1944 Education Act. The Butler Act, named after the Conservative politician Rab Butler, committed the Government to providing free secondary education. The Act set up a **tripartite** system of grammar schools, technical schools and secondary modern schools designed to teach different skills. An exam known as the '11 plus' determined which school students would attend.

Labour's 'New Jerusalem'

During the 1945 election campaign, Labour leader Clement Attlee set out Labour's vision of a **'New Jerusalem'**. His priorities for post-war Britain were to:

- achieve full employment
- address social inequalities by implementing a comprehensive system of social insurance
- nationalise key industries
- resolve Britain's balance of payments problems
- solve the problem of homelessness by building 400,000 new houses a year.

Mind map

Use the information on the opposite page to add detail to the mind map below.

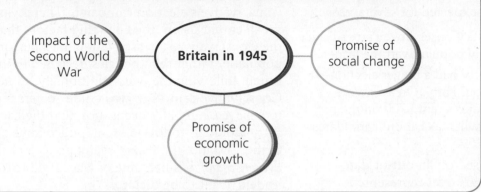

Linking sources

Below are a sample exam-style part (a) question and the three sources referred to in the question. In one colour, draw links between the sources to show ways in which they agree about reactions to the 1944 Education Act. In another colour, draw links between the sources to show ways in which they disagree.

Study Sources 1, 2 and 3.

How far do Sources 2 and 3 support the view presented in Source 1 that the 1944 Education Act was 'a great step forward'?

SOURCE 1

(From the Western Morning News*, 7 December 1944)*

'The [Education] Act means a great step forward in making us an educational democracy,' said Mr B. G. Lampard-Vachell, chairman of the Devon Higher Education Committee, speaking at Torquay Grammar School for Girls yesterday. [However] … implementing the new Act was going to take many years and needed the goodwill of all. Until they had teachers and buildings it could not be done, and they would therefore need a good deal of money from the Treasury.

SOURCE 2

(From a report of a meeting of the North Dorset Conservatives, taken from the Western Gazette*, 18 August 1944)*

[Captain Hambro said] the new Education Act was very fine, no doubt, and badly wanted, but throughout it there was not a word about the parents. Where were they getting to? After all, there was such a thing as a father and mother. Yet the children, as far as he could see, were going to be taken from the cradle to the grave and handled by the State, and the responsibility of the parents ignored. He was certain that was not required by the vast majority of the people.

SOURCE 3

(From an editorial in The Times*, 31 March 1945)*

Tomorrow the greater part of the new Education Act comes into operation. In present circumstances no spectacular transformation can be expected as an immediate result. The changeover from the old to the new system of public education will [need] manpower and materials. But however small the immediate effect, the event is nevertheless momentous.

The Labour election victory of 1945

In 1945, Labour won a landslide election victory. Labour's victory was unexpected for several reasons.

- Winston Churchill, the Conservative Party's leader, had been an extremely popular wartime leader.
- The Conservative Party had a bigger election budget than the Labour Party. On average, Conservative candidates spent £780 on their election campaigns, whereas Labour candidates spent an average of £595.
- The election was based on an out-of-date electoral register which over-represented older voters who tended to support the Conservatives.

Nonetheless, the Labour Party gained an overall majority in the House of Commons.

Party	Percentage of vote in 1945	Seats in Parliament in 1945
Labour	47.8	393
Conservative	39.8	213
Liberal	9	12

The reasons for the Labour landslide

Perceptions of the Conservatives

In spite of Churchill's popularity as a wartime leader, the majority of the public were unenthusiastic about the Conservative Party.

- Voters associated the Conservative Party with the **interwar depression**, believing that interwar Conservative Governments had failed to solve Britain's economic and social problems.
- The Conservatives were unpopular because they had backed the policy of **appeasement** rather than standing up to Hitler in the late 1930s.
- Voters tended to view the Conservatives as a party for, and made up of, the rich and privileged.
- Many older voters blamed the Conservatives for failing to build **'a land fit for heroes'** following the end of the First World War.

Additionally, there were problems with the Conservative's election campaign. There was too much emphasis on 'the Churchill factor', that is, the Conservatives stressed Churchill's personal popularity rather than policies designed to improve Britain following the war. Additionally, some of the Conservative campaign was crude. Voters refused to believe Churchill's accusation that the Labour Party would introduce a secret police force similar to the Gestapo (the Nazi's secret police), or the *Evening Standard*'s headline of May 1945 that Labour leaders 'want to be dictators'.

Perceptions of Labour

The Labour Party benefited from the public desire for change. A 1945 **Gallup poll** showed that 56 per cent of voters wanted extensive change. This helped Labour because voters tended to see the Conservatives as the party of the past and Labour as the party most likely to introduce radical reform.

Labour's manifesto, entitled *Let us Face the Future*, was also closer to the public's desire for a more egalitarian Britain. Opinion polls showed that there was an increasing desire for equality of opportunity (the principle that everyone should have the same chance to succeed) in Britain. Voters tended to believe that the Labour Party was more likely to introduce policies that helped ordinary people rather than protecting the privileges of the rich.

The Labour leadership also won widespread respect during the Second World War, particularly Attlee (wartime Deputy Prime Minister), Herbert Morrison (wartime Home Secretary) and Ernest Bevin (wartime Minister of Labour).

Finally, the Labour Party had a significant electoral advantage. The **First Past the Post** electoral system, and the distribution of Labour's vote meant that Labour needed fewer votes to win each seat than the Conservatives. On average, Conservatives needed around 46,000 votes to win a seat, whereas Labour only needed 30,500 votes.

Add own knowledge

Below are a sample exam-style part (b) question and the three sources referred to in the question. In one colour, draw links between the sources to show ways in which they agree about the importance of the Labour Party election campaign. In another colour, draw links between the sources to show ways in which they disagree. Around the edge of the sources, write relevant own knowledge. Again, draw links to show the ways in which this agrees and disagrees with the sources.

Use Sources 1, 2 and 3 and your own knowledge.

Do you agree with the view that the Labour Party election campaign was responsible for the victory of the Labour Party in the 1945 general election?

SOURCE 1

(From the Labour Party election manifesto, 1945)

The nation needs a tremendous overhaul, a great programme of modernisation and re-equipment of its homes, its factories and machinery, its schools, its social services. All parties say so – the Labour Party means it … the Labour Party will put the community first and the sectional interests of private business after.

SOURCE 3

(From Kevin Jefferys, The Churchill Coalition and Wartime Politics, published 1995)

The 1945 result must be set against the background of Labour's increased wartime popularity. [However], if the 'people's war' had made a Labour victory certain by the time of Germany's surrender, Churchill made matters worse by his disastrous handling of the election campaign.

SOURCE 2

(From Chris Rowe, Britain 1929–1998, published 2004)

It is difficult to believe that the 1945 electoral campaign could have decided the outcome of the election, though it might have increased the margin of victory. Labour's landslide was by such a decisive margin that it was almost certainly a foregone conclusion before electioneering even started. Even so, it should not be forgotten that, at the time, many people – both delighted Labour supporters and shocked Conservatives – were astonished by the result.

 Spectrum of significance

Below are a sample exam-style part (b) question and a list of general points which could be used to answer the question. Use your own knowledge and the information on the opposite page to reach a judgement about the importance of these general points to the question posed. Write numbers on the spectrum below to indicate their relative importance. Having done this, write a brief justification of your placement, explaining why some of these factors are more important than others. The resulting diagram could form the basis of an essay plan.

Do you agree with the view that the Labour Party election campaign was responsible for the victory of the Labour Party in the 1945 general election?

1. Strengths of the Labour Party election campaign
2. Public perceptions of the Conservative Party
3. Weaknesses of the Conservative Party election campaign
4. Labour leadership during the Second World War
5. Labour Party electoral advantage

Very important ⟷ Less important

Labour's social policy

Clement Attlee's Labour Government created the modern welfare state, and introduced legislation which tried to ensure all citizens were entitled to receive a minimum standard of care.

Social security

Labour attempted to produce a 'national minimum' standard of living through a series of laws, establishing new **economic rights**. The Beveridge Report had proposed many of these (see page 4). They included the following:

- The Family Allowances Act (1945), which provided child benefit for each child, other than the eldest. The wartime coalition Government passed this Act, but it came into force under the Labour Government of 1945–1951.

- The Industrial Injuries Act (1946), which provided financial cover for people who were injured at work.

- The National Insurance Act (1946), which established a **universal system of benefits**, including unemployment benefit, sickness benefit, maternity benefit and a pension. These were funded by compulsory National Insurance contributions made by employers, workers and the Government.

- The National Assistance Act (1948), which abolished the **poor law** and established a **welfare safety net** for all living in poverty such as the long-term homeless, those unable to work due to disability and single parents.

Housing

According to opinion polls in 1945, voters said new housing was top priority. The government passed the New Towns Act of 1946 and the Town and Country Planning Act of 1947, and aimed to build 400,000 new homes every year – although shortages of labour, materials and money meant that only 230,000 homes were built in 1948.

Health and education

The National Health Service Act (1946) established government provision of healthcare, **free at the point of delivery**. It came into effect in July 1948 and brought all existing hospitals run by local authorities and charities together into a national network, the National Health Service (NHS).

Attlee's Government also implemented the Butler Act (1944) (see page 4). In 1947, the Government raised the school leaving age to 15. Labour's Education Secretaries tended to have an elitist attitude to education. They prioritised the needs of grammar schools and neglected the needs of secondary modern schools. Nonetheless, overall the Government recruited 25,000 new teachers and increased spending on education.

The impact of the welfare state

Labour succeeded in establishing a universal right to a minimum standard of living. However, the National Insurance Act provided flat rate benefits that did not account for the cost of living. The benefits provided were often so small that, by 1951, 2.5 million working people had to rely on benefits from the National Assistance Act.

Labour's record on housing was mixed. Attlee did not implement his election promise of establishing a Ministry of Housing. Therefore, on becoming Minister of Health, Aneurin Bevan was responsible for health and housing. Bevan tended to prioritise health reform and neglect housing. By 1951, Attlee's Government had built around 1 million new homes but a 1951 government report showed that 750,000 families were still without adequate housing.

The NHS was highly successful in terms of meeting medical need. In its first year, it employed 18,000 general practitioners (GPs) who wrote 187,000 prescriptions, treated 8.5 million dental patients and distributed 5.25 million pairs of glasses. However, the NHS cost £250 million (double the estimated cost) and therefore Bevan's Cabinet colleagues demanded cuts. As a result, and to fund military action in the Korean War, the Government introduced charges for glasses and dental work to save money.

Eliminate irrelevance

Below are a sample exam-style part (b) question and a paragraph written in answer to this question. The question refers to Source 1 above, and Sources 2 and 3 below. Read the paragraph and identify parts of the paragraph that are not directly relevant to the question. Draw a line through the information that is irrelevant and justify your deletions in the margin.

Use Sources 1, 2 and 3 and your own knowledge.

Do you agree with the view that the social reforms of the Labour Governments in the years 1945–1951 were successful at reducing social inequalities?

There is evidence in all three sources to suggest that there were limitations to the extent to which the Labour Governments in the years 1945–1951 were successful at reducing social inequalities. Source 3 acknowledges the successes of the reforms, but states that 'much more remains to be done'. This is taken from the Labour Party manifesto of 1951, and provides evidence that the Government itself was aware of the limitations of its reforms. Indeed, by 1951, the number of people reliant on the benefits offered by the National Assistance Act was 2.5 million, indicating that a significant proportion of the population were still living in poverty. Sources 1 and 2 provide further examples of the limitations of the reforms. Source 1 notes that 'the principle of universal benefits meant disproportionate gains for middle-class families'. This source was written by the historian Kevin Jefferys in 1992 and so will be an accurate description of what happened. In addition, Source 2 explains that 'the Chancellor of the Exchequer was obliged to reintroduce charges for NHS false teeth and glasses'. This was a response to the high costs of the NHS (£250 million – double that anticipated) but meant that the poorest people did not have access to all health services. One of the reasons the Government could not afford the NHS was because of the Korean War, which was fought from 1950–1953. In this way, the social reforms of the Labour Governments of 1945–1951 were not entirely successful at reducing social inequalities as they did not eradicate poverty, and did not benefit the rich and poor equally.

SOURCE 1

(From Kevin Jefferys, The Attlee Governments, *published 1992)*

Within eighteen months, Attlee's Cabinet had done more than any previous twentieth-century government to improve the lot of ordinary working people. Although the principle of universal benefits meant disproportionate gains for middle-class families, for the majority of the population welfare reform after 1945 offered free medical treatment, subsidised housing and education opportunities on a scale not known before.

SOURCE 2

(From an article in the Guardian, *published 14 March 2001)*

The Government was forced to retreat from its first grand vision of free, comprehensive health care for all. In the beginning, everything was provided … But with Britain showing few signs of economic take off, the budgetary burden was enormous. In 1951, the Chancellor of the Exchequer was obliged to reintroduce charges for NHS false teeth and glasses. Aneurin Bevan … stormed out of government.

SOURCE 3

(From the Labour Party manifesto, 1951)

Contrast Britain in the inter-war years with Britain to-day. Then we had mass unemployment; mass fear; mass misery. Now we have full employment. Then millions suffered from insecurity and want. Now we have social security for every man, woman and child. Then dread of doctors' bills was a nightmare in countless homes. Now we have a national health scheme. There has, indeed, been progress, but much more remains to be done.

Labour's economic policy

Between 1945 and 1951, Labour created a mixed economy. High levels of state ownership and government intervention existed alongside **private enterprise**. Government policy reflected the key priorities of creating full employment and solving Britain's **balance of payments deficit**.

Nationalisation

Labour nationalised the following key industries by 1949:

Date	Act	Industry/service nationalised
1946	Coal Industry Nationalisation Act	Coal mining
1946	Bank of England Act	Bank of England
1947	Transport Act	Railways Road haulage Busses
1947	Electricity Act	Electricity
1948	Gas Act	Gas
1949	Iron and Steel Act	Iron and steel

In essence, the Government bought the industries from their existing owners, paying:

- £164 million for the coal mines
- £1000 million for the rail network
- £540 million for electricity companies
- £265 million for gas companies.

Reasons for nationalisation

Many Labour members felt **nationalisation** achieved the goal of establishing 'the common ownership of the means of production', as set out in clause IV of the Labour constitution. Additionally, Labour leaders hoped to ensure full employment by controlling key industries and the Bank of England. Unions hoped workers would come to control nationalised industries, or at least their rights would be protected.

The dollar crisis

In 1945, Labour faced its first major economic problem. The massive cost of the war left Britain economically dependent on the USA. However, President Truman decided to end US economic aid as he did not want to help fund the new socialist Government. Without US support, Britain faced bankruptcy. Consequently, the new Government was forced to negotiate the Anglo-American Loan. The loan gave the British Government $6000 million. In return, the USA demanded that Britain should make sterling fully **convertible** to dollars by mid-1947. This triggered the dollar crisis of 1947. Anticipating that the price of the pound would decline, foreign countries sold their stocks of sterling. Britain was forced to buy sterling to stabilise the price, which cost £645 million during 1947–1949. In 1949, the Government devalued the pound and, on 18 September 1949, the exchange rate dropped from $1:£4.08 to $1:£2.80.

Austerity

Britain had a large balance of payments deficit from the war. The Government continued wartime austerity measures, such as food rationing, to try to solve this. Rationing goods meant that Britain could import less and export more. Under Stafford Cripps, Labour Chancellor from 1947–1950, post-war rationing was more severe than wartime rationing. For example, in 1946 bread was rationed for the first time. Labour also tried to control imports by agreeing a wage freeze with major trade unions in 1948.

How successful was Labour's economic policy?

Britain's economy certainly grew in the period 1945–1951.

- Between 1945 and 1951, industrial production increased by 33 per cent.
- Between 1948 and 1950, the economy grew by 4 per cent a year.
- Britain's labour productivity reached an all-time high in 1950.
- Between 1945 and 1950, exports increased by 77 per cent.
- By 1948, Britain no longer had a balance of payments deficit.
- Britain's share of world trade grew from 17.5 per cent in 1939 to 20.7 per cent in 1950.
- Full employment was achieved: between 1947 and 1951, unemployment never rose above 300,000.

However, in terms of nationalisation, opportunities were undoubtedly missed. There were very few attempts to reform government-controlled industries, and therefore inefficiencies continued. Furthermore, after spending such large sums on nationalising key industries, the Government had less money available to invest in industrial modernisation.

Below are a sample exam-style part (a) question and two paragraphs written in answer to this question. Read the question and the two answers, as well as the sources. Then, using a highlighter, highlight examples of integration – where sources are used together. You cannot reach Level 3 or Level 4 of the part (a) mark scheme (see page 78) without integration of the sources. Which paragraph reaches the higher level?

Study Sources 1, 2 and 3.

How far do the sources suggest that the policy of bread rationing, introduced in 1946, met with opposition from the public?

Sample 1

There is evidence in all three sources that the policy of bread rationing met with opposition from the public. Sources 2 and 3 both refer to petitions against the rationing: Source 2 states that 'a million signatures' had been collected by the British Housewives' League, while Source 3 refers to 'many Members of Parliament who have had to present petitions'. Additionally, Source 1 states that there is 'genuine bewilderment among large sections of the people', supporting the suggestion in both Sources 2 and 3 that opposition was widespread. Furthermore, Sources 2 and 3 provide specific examples of opposition to bread rationing in the form of 'Mrs Irene Lovelock, president of the British Housewives League', mentioned in Source 2, and the 'baker' and the 'lady' referred to in Source 3. In this way, collectively, the sources provide evidence of public opposition to bread rationing.

Sample 2

Source 1 provides evidence that the policy of bread rationing met with opposition from the public. The source describes 'genuine bewilderment among large sections of the people', and states that 'the Government must be prepared for a more critical public'. Source 2 provides evidence of criticism from the public, referring to 'the growing resentment of British housewives at the bread ration'. Furthermore, it states that the British Housewives' League has collected 'a million signatures on a petition' against the bread ration. This indicates the extent of the opposition. Finally, Source 3 refers to 'many Members of Parliament who have had to present petitions [against rationing]', suggesting that opposition was widespread.

SOURCE 1

(From the Guardian, 28 June 1946)

The Government must realise that, besides the unscrupulous political twist which some Conservatives and their papers are giving to the food problem, there is genuine bewilderment among large sections of the people. We shall have to see how the scheme works out. But the Government must be prepared for a more critical public.

SOURCE 3

(From a speech by the Labour MP John Leslie in the House of Commons, 18 July 1946)

I may be more fortunate than many Members of Parliament who have had to present petitions. So far, I have had only two letters, one from a baker and the other from a lady. People in my constituency are not behind in presenting petitions; I have received petitions from villages about the lack of water supplies and about medical services. I have also had petitions from farmers about the use of a water mill, but I have had no petitions about bread rationing. The people in my constituency believe that it is the fairest way, and that everyone will get a fair share.

SOURCE 2

(From The Sydney Morning Herald, 1 July 1946)

There are indications that Cabinet is perturbed by the growing resentment of British housewives at the bread ration. The newly-formed British Housewives' League is expected to present a million signatures on a petition against rationing to the Government. It is believed that several members of the Government opposed the bread rationing decision, and it is thought the next three months will be a most critical period for the Labour Administration.

Mrs Irene Lovelock, president of the British Housewives League, declared that the Cabinet had no conception of housewives' difficulties.

'They think we are whining and so they are determined we must just take it,' she said. 'We will not take it.'

The role of Clement Attlee and Labour's critics

Man of the people

Attlee was not a gifted public speaker, and, worse still, sometimes gave speeches without wearing his false teeth. However, he had an ordinariness about him that appealed to working-class voters. As Prime Minister he liked to use public transport where possible. For example, when opening a cinema in London's East End in 1947 he travelled to and from the event by bus. Moreover, Attlee's down-to-earth style helped to make the radicalism of some of the new Government's measures less threatening for many voters.

However, by 1951, Attlee's sensible style was less appealing. Bevan noted that after six years the public had come to associate the Labour Government with 'greyness and dullness'. Attlee represented both.

Attlee and the establishment

Attlee's natural sympathy for the British establishment meant that there were limits to the Government's radicalism. Attlee respected the system of British government and admired George VI. Therefore, he was unwilling to support wide-ranging constitutional reform. For example, in 1950 Attlee refused to be pressured into giving a greater measure of self-government to Scotland.

Additionally, Attlee's rather traditional outlook meant that he failed to recognise the significance of movements in France and Germany towards European integration. Consequently, the Government missed the opportunity of putting Britain at the heart of moves towards the creation of the **European Economic Community**. By contrast, Attlee was committed to retaining close links with the USA and sent troops to support the USA during the Korean War, the first military conflict of the Cold War.

Party unity

Attlee was good at managing the different personalities in his Government. The Cabinet was dominated by Bevan, Cripps and Morrison. Bevan, on the left, was continually pushing for more spending on projects like the NHS. Cripps and Morrison, on the right, wanted to keep control of spending and, after 1948, stopped advocating major reform. From 1945 to 1950, Attlee was able to manage these different visions and ensure a high degree of unity but, by 1951, this became increasingly difficult. Attlee was unable to prevent Bevan's resignation when he stepped down as Minister for Health in protest at the introduction of charges for glasses and dental work.

Criticisms of Attlee

Attlee's Government faced criticism from Labour's supporters on the Left, and from the Conservatives and their supporters on the Right.

Left-wing Labour members were critical of Attlee's approach to nationalisation. They argued that the Government should have placed nationalised industries under workers' control, whereas Attlee left the management of nationalised industries unreformed. The Left was also critical of Attlee's decision to support the USA during the Korean War, arguing that entering the war was extremely expensive and government money would have been better spent on welfare and healthcare.

The Conservatives were critical of some aspects of nationalisation. They opposed the nationalisation of iron and steel. They argued that nationalisation had not significantly improved the coal or transport industry and therefore steel was best left in the **private sector**. The sugar manufacturers Tate and Lyle also ran a successful campaign to stop the nationalisation of the sugar industry. The campaign featured the slogan 'Tate not state' and a cartoon sugar cube called Mr Cube.

Doing reliability well

Below are a series of definitions listing common reasons why sources are either reliable or unreliable, and two sources. Under each source, explain why the source is either reliable or unreliable for the purpose stated, justifying your answer by referring to the following definitions.

- **Vested interest**: the source is written so that the writer can protect their power or their financial interests.
- **Second-hand report**: the writer of the source is not an eyewitness, but is relying on someone else's account.
- **Expertise**: the source is written on a subject on which the author (for example, a historian) is an expert.
- **Political bias**: a source is written by a politician and it reflects their political views.
- **Reputation**: a source is written to protect the writer's reputation.

SOURCE 1

(Part of a Parliamentary speech given by the Conservative MP Cyril Osborne, September 1950)

The hon. Gentleman is making the point that the steel workers will work better, and continue to work better, because the industry is owned by the nation. Would he not agree that in the first two weeks after the coal mining industry was taken over there was a great spurt of production, but that subsequently production fell, and that the first zest did not last more than a month?

> The source is reliable/unreliable as a description of the impact of the nationalisation of the coal industry because
>
> _____
>
> _____

SOURCE 2

(From Robert Pearce, Attlee's Labour Governments 1945–51, *published 2002)*

By 1951, Labour's nationalisation was complete. To some this was far too much, for to their minds nationalisation was associated with loss-making: no one believed that the mines could be run profitably. In fact coal output rose significantly from 1946 to 1951, by which time productivity had never been higher. Fatal accidents in the mines were far fewer than ever before in 1948, and fewer still in 1949.

> The source is reliable/unreliable as a description of the impact of the nationalisation of the coal industry because
>
> _____
>
> _____

Recommended reading

Below is a list of suggested further reading on this topic.

- *Britain 1945–2007*, pages 1–30, Michael Lynch (2008)
- *Britain Since 1945: The People's Peace,* pages 29–71, Kenneth O. Morgan (2001)
- *British Political History, 1867–2001: Democracy and Decline*, pages 443–456, Malcolm L. Pearce and Geoffrey Stewart (1991)

Age of austerity?

This period is often remembered as an age of austerity due to continued food rationing, and the limited availability of consumer goods and leisure opportunities. Nonetheless, by 1951, Britain was seeing the first glimpses of a consumer society.

Standard of living

The working class

The standard of living for most working people improved during the period 1945–1951, through the combination of full employment, increased welfare, low **inflation** and, from 1948, increasing economic growth. By 1950, working class incomes had risen by 9 per cent.

Poverty was also significantly reduced. For example, according to the Rowntree Foundation, an organisation known for its research on poverty and housing in Britain, poverty in York decreased from 17.7 per cent of the population in 1936 to 2.8 per cent in 1950.

The middle class

The middle class benefited less from Labour policies. While some middle-class families benefited from a free grammar school education, which meant they did not have to pay for places at private schools, many felt their standard of living had been hit by the lack of availability of consumer goods, furniture, petrol and cars. Middle class incomes fell by 7 per cent between 1938 and 1950.

Rationing

While rationing continued throughout this period, the restrictions relaxed towards the end. In 1948, the Government used some of the $3000 million it gained in **Marshall Aid** to ensure that rations were maintained at their established level. The Government estimated that without Marshall Aid, rations would have been cut by 33 per cent. In November 1948, the President of the Board of Trade, Harold Wilson, announced the 'bonfire of controls' and abolished the rationing of toys, cutlery and pens. By April 1949, bread, sweets and chocolate were no longer rationed.

Leisure

In spite of Cripp's austerity measures there were some leisure opportunities. Between 1945 and 1951:

- attendance at football and cricket matches reached record numbers
- 1635 million cinema tickets were sold
- half a million people took a holiday at Butlins, a chain of holiday camps across Britain, every year.

The 1948 Local Government Act also permitted local authorities to raise money for public entertainment such as drama, music or dancing.

The Festival of Britain

The Festival of Britain, held throughout the summer of 1951, was a clear attempt to break with austerity. The festival attempted to promote exports by celebrating British design and industry, and was open to the public, giving working people a glimpse of cutting edge design.

The South Bank Exhibition was the centrepiece of the festival. It featured the futuristic Dome of Discovery, the Telecinema (which showed films in 3D) and the first performances of steelpan music in Britain, thanks to Trinidad's All Steel Percussion Orchestra. Exhibitions showed new fashion and interior design ideas. Further down the Thames, at the Festival Pleasure Gardens in Battersea, the festival became a huge funfair. More than 8 million people attended the South Bank Exhibition during the summer of 1951.

A special housing project was built as part of the festival: the Lansbury Estate in Tower Hamlets. This was an attempt to build urban housing designed to support the needs of a modern community. Like the rest of the festival, it was intended to be a window to the future.

RAG – Rate the timeline

Below are a sample exam-style part (b) question and a timeline. Read the question, study the timeline and, using three coloured pens, put a red, amber or green star next to the events to show:

- **Red:** Events and policies that have no relevance to the question
- **Amber:** Events and policies that have some significance to the question
- **Green:** Events and policies that are directly relevant to the question

1) Do you agree with the view that the social reforms of the Labour Governments in the years 1945–1951 reduced social inequalities?

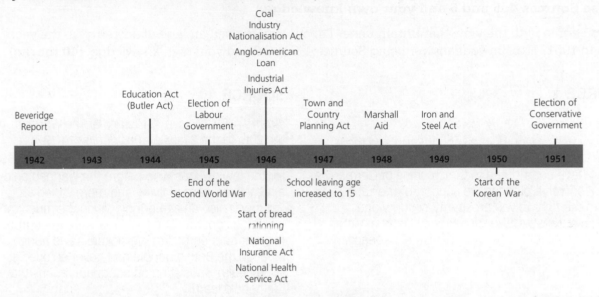

Write the question

The following sources relate to the effect of Labour Government policies on life in Britain in the period 1945–1951. Read the guidance detailing what you need to know about this topic. Having done this, write an exam-style part (b) question using the sources.

SOURCE 1

(From Michael Lynch, Britain 1945–2007, *published 2008)*

Attlee's government inherited crushing financial difficulties in 1945. To meet this crisis the Chancellor of the Exchequer negotiated a loan from the USA. The government's hope was that the loan would provide the basis of an industrial recovery. But such recovery as did occur was never enough to meet expectations. The hard times were made harder by the coinciding of this period of austerity with Labour's creation of the welfare state, which placed further heavy financial burdens on an already strained economy.

SOURCE 2

(From Graham P. Thomas, Government and the Economy Today, *published 1992)*

[From 1946] working class people grumbled but accepted rationing as a system of 'fair shares'. Social reforms such as school meals and better medical services improved standards of health; poverty declined and full employment and a low rate of inflation helped those on low incomes.

SOURCE 3

(From the diary of Rose Uttin, a housewife living in Wembley. She is describing a day in 1947)

No soap to be bought anywhere. Lily sent me 2 lbs of potatoes through the post & I am saving them for Sunday's dinner. Last night I went to the Red House to play cards in my fur coat and turban it was so cold there.

Section 1: Exam focus

On pages 17–19 are sample answers to the exam-style questions on this page. Read the answers and the examiner comments around them.

a) Study Sources 1, 2 and 3.

How far do Sources 1, 2 and 3 agree that the Labour Party won the 1945 general election due to its commitment to 'winning the peace'? Explain your answer using the evidence of Sources 1, 2 and 3. **(20 marks)**

b) Use Sources 4, 5 and 6 and your own knowledge.

Do you agree with the view that Britain under Labour experienced an 'age of austerity' in the years 1945 to 1951? Explain your answer using Sources 4, 5 and 6 and your own knowledge. **(40 marks)**

SOURCE 1

(From The Times, *11 May 1945)*

A victory declaration by the Labour Party and the Trades Union Congress acknowledges the services of all who have contributed to the crushing of Germany's military power. It pledges the support of the Labour Party to the fight to win prosperity, security and happiness. It states, 'We salute the winning of victory in war. We call for the winning of victory in peace.'

SOURCE 2

(From Winston Churchill's Declaration of Policy to the Electors – *The Conservative Party manifesto for the 1945 general election)*

Ours is a great nation and never in its history has it stood in higher repute in the world than today. In recent generations, enormous material progress has been made. That progress must be extended and accelerated not by subordinating the individual to the authority of the State. Our programme is not based upon unproved theories or fine phrases, but upon principles that have been tested anew in the fires of war and not found wanting.

SOURCE 3

(From an article in LIFE *magazine, 25 June 1945)*

With Churchill, the Tories expect to win by at least 60 seats in Parliament. The polls say so. So according to report, does Labour leader Clement Attlee. The Labour Party's programme is socialism. It would nationalise coal, iron, steel and transport. The ex-truck drivers, boiler makers and clerks who lead Labour, though perhaps less posh than the Tories, are not short of brain or courage. Their big leaders did huge jobs in the war. Churchill promises employment, and special help for small businesses. He warns that a Labour regime will be 'a sort of Gestapo'.

SOURCE 4

(From J.A.S. Grenville, A History Of The World: from the 20th to the 21st Century, *published 1994)*

The early post-war years were an 'age of austerity' for the few millions who before the war had enjoyed a higher standard of living and more varied food. But it was also an age during which the much more numerous poor for the first time were freed from the fear of unemployment, sickness and hunger. As a nation the British people had never enjoyed such good health, subsisting on adequate rations that kept the people lean.

SOURCE 5

(From Tony Jud, Postwar: A History of Europe Since 1945, *published 2006)*

The government publicly celebrated a 'bonfire of controls' in 1948. But many of those same controls had to be re-imposed during the Korean War. Basic food rationing in Britain only ended in 1954, long after the rest of Western Europe. In the words of one English housewife, 'It was queues for everything ...' However, beginning in 1951, it seemed as though the worst of the austerity years were over. The country offered itself the optimistic 'Festival of Britain'.

SOURCE 6

(From an article published in The Times, *6 February 1946)*

Sir Ben Smith, the Minister of Food, announced in the House of Commons yesterday a reduction in the food ration. The weekly fat ration will be reduced by one ounce, white bread will be replaced by a darker loaf, and less animal feed will lead to smaller supplies of bacon, poultry and eggs. Powdered eggs will also be withdrawn from sale and restaurants will be restricted from serving bread. The Minister, however, stated that his one desire was to avoid the rationing of bread.

a) Study Sources 1, 2 and 3.

How far do Sources 1, 2 and 3 agree that the Labour Party won the 1945 general election due to its commitment to 'winning the peace'? Explain your answer, using the evidence of Sources 1, 2 and 3. **(20 marks)**

There is evidence in all three sources that the Labour Party won the 1945 election due to its commitment to 'win the peace'. Source 1 explicitly uses the phrase, Source 2 implicitly attacks Labour's plans for post-war Britain and Source 3 outlines several of the policies that the Labour Party campaigned for in the 1945 election.

The introduction begins with a clear focus on the issue raised in the question.

Source 1 implies that winning the peace was a significant factor in the Labour victory. The source, which reports Labour's victory declaration, states, 'We call for the winning of victory in peace'. Source 3 supports this by showing the detail of Labour's proposals for 'winning the peace'. These include the nationalisation of 'coal, iron, steel and transport'. These were, as the source implies, policies that reflected the fact that the Labour leadership 'are not short of brain or courage'. Source 2 supports the importance of this aspect of Labour's plan as it attacks Labour for 'subordinating the individual to the authority of the State'. This is an implicit attack on nationalisation, which brought private industry under state control. Clearly, Labour's commitment to 'winning the peace' was important to their victory as it appealed to the public's desire for bold new policies.

The candidate begins this paragraph with the best evidence available that Labour won the 1945 election due to its commitment to win the peace.

However, the sources also point to other factors that helped Labour win. First, Sources 2 and 3 indicate that the Conservatives had lost their appeal. Source 2, an extract from their manifesto, emphasises that 'enormous material progress has been made'. This implies that the Conservatives, unlike Labour in Source 1, were not appealing to the desire for change. The title of Source 2, Winston Churchill's 'Declaration of Policy to the Electors', also emphasises the past by implicitly emphasising Churchill's reputation as a great wartime leader. Finally, Source 3 points to a significant difference between the Conservatives and Labour. It argues: 'The ex-truck drivers, boiler makers and clerks who lead Labour, though perhaps less posh than the Tories, are not short of brain or courage'. This indicates that one reason for Labour's popularity was that while the Conservatives were associated with the past and with privileged people, Labour won the election because they were associated with working people. This is supported by Source 1, which is a joint statement by 'the Labour Party and the Trades Union Congress', which represented working people. Source 3's reference to Churchill's claim that 'a Labour regime will be "a sort of Gestapo"' is further evidence that the Conservatives ran a poor campaign. The emphasis of tradition in the Conservative's manifesto (Source 2) helps explain why the Conservatives lost and Labour won.

This paragraph immediately highlights a similarity between Sources 2 and 3, and therefore continues the clear comparison started earlier in the essay.

There is some attempt to understand the sources in the context that they have been written by referring to the failures of the Conservative campaign. However, they are not used to evaluate the reliability of the sources.

In conclusion, the sources agree to a fair extent that Labour's commitment to winning the peace was the main reason for Labour's election victory. However, they also point to the fact that the Conservatives fought a poor campaign which did not appeal to the desires of British voters in 1945.

The conclusion summarises the essay, but does not really address 'how far' the sources support the statement in the question.

14/20

This essay gets a mark high in Level 3, because although it compares the sources in detail, it does not really address their reliability, nor does it focus on 'how far' they support the statement in the question.

Moving from Level 3 to Level 4

The exam focus Part (a) essays at the end of Sections 2, 3 and 4 (pages 33, 51 and 69) have been awarded Level 4. Read all of the essays and examiner's comments. Make a list of the extra features required to push this Part (a) Level 3 essay into Level 4, and rewrite so that it reaches Level 4.

b) Use Sources 4, 5 and 6 and your own knowledge.

Do you agree with the view that Britain under Labour experienced an 'age of austerity' in the years 1945 to 1951? Explain your answer, using Sources 4, 5 and 6 and your own knowledge. **(40 marks)**

Between 1945 and 1951, Britain under Labour certainly experienced an 'age of austerity'. However, as Source 4 argues, the austerity was at its worst in the 'early post-war years', and by the late 1940s, there were signs that austerity was fading. Indeed, as Source 5 argues, by 1951 there was a national feeling of optimism about the future. Finally, although it is mainly right to say that Britain between 1945 and 1951 did experience an 'age of austerity', it was austerity with a purpose.

Source 4 clearly argues that Britain experienced an age of austerity after the Second World War. Specifically, for middle-class people, 'who before the war had enjoyed a higher standard of living', the post-war years of rationing were hard. The middle class were not helped by Labour's social security legislation, such as the National Insurance Act or the Industrial Injuries Act 1946, or the National Assistance Act of 1948. However, they were affected by continued rationing, which was worse under Stafford Cripps than it had been during the war. Source 6 shows that rationing got worse after the war. It quotes the Minister of Food stating that 'the fat ration will be reduced ... white bread will be replaced by a darker loaf'. What is worse is that he broke his pledge, as the end of the source states, to avoid bread rationing. In fact, bread rationing was introduced for the first time in 1946. Therefore, Source 4 is correct when it argues that the middle class had less varied food than it did before the war. In this way, the Government's policy of continued rationing meant that Britain did experience an age of austerity, as for many living standards were worse in the period 1945 to 1951 than they had been before the war.

Nonetheless, Source 4 also argues that the austerity helped improve the lives of working people. It claims that 1945 to 1951 'was also an age during which the much more numerous poor for the first time were freed from the fear of unemployment, sickness and hunger'. Indeed, the Government brought in austerity measures to ensure that it could also introduce policies to help the working class. Rationing meant that the Government could use more of the nation's resources to develop social services and education. For example, it allowed the Government to implement the 1944 Butler Act, establish the National Health Service in 1948 and build 1 million new homes. Austerity meant that inflation stayed low and the economy could grow. The working class benefited from this as by 1950 working class income had risen by 9 per cent. Some impoverished areas benefited greatly from Labour's post-war policies. Poverty in York, for example, decreased from 17.7 per cent of the population in 1936 to 2.8 per cent of the population in 1950. Finally, although rationing continued, the Government used some of the $3000 million granted

The introduction begins with a clear focus on the issue raised in the question.

The paragraph contains a great deal of own knowledge, which is consistently integrated with the sources. It distinguishes analytically between the extent to which different groups experienced austerity, and between the early years and the later years of the Labour Government.

In addition, these paragraphs continue the focus on how different groups experienced austerity, distinguishing between the working class and the middle class.

The argument is supported by accurate and relevant own knowledge.

in Marshall Aid to ensure that rationing never fell below a reasonable level. In fact, as Source 4 argues, 'As a nation the British people had never enjoyed such good health, subsisting on adequate rations that kept the people lean.'

Source 5 argues that by the end of the period austerity was coming to an end. It argues that 'beginning in 1951, it seemed as though the worst of the austerity years were over. Indeed, the Festival of Britain was a clear break with austerity. It emphasised high quality consumer goods and leisure. The Festival featured a Telecinema, which showed 3D films, a funfair and the first performances of steelpan music in Britain, by Trinidad's All Steel Percussion Orchestra. However, Source 5, in contrast to Source 4, argues that the break with austerity came late in the period. It argues that even the 'bonfire of controls' of 1949, which ended the rationing of toys, cutlery and pens, failed to end austerity. This is because 'many of those same controls had to be re-imposed during the Korean War'. Therefore, it is mainly true that between 1945 and 1951 Britain experienced an age of austerity because rationing was still in place as late as 1951.

In conclusion, Source 6 paints a bleak picture of Britain in the middle of an age of austerity, which is not surprising as the source was written in 1446, the year when bread rationing was introduced and therefore at the height of Labour's austerity. Source 5 shows that austerity continued right up until the end of the Labour Government in 1951. Nonetheless, by 1949 the 'bonfire of controls' showed that the Government was trying to reduce austerity and the 1951 Festival of Britain was a window on to a more prosperous future. However, Source 4 is correct to argue that austerity was felt mainly by the middle class and that for the working people of Britain the post-war period of full employment and the welfare state was a time of security even if rationing was still continuing.

> Here, the candidate weighs the evidence presented in Source 5 by noting the period the source is referring to and contrasting it to Source 4.

> The conclusion uses all three sources to reach an overall judgement that reflects the argument of the essay.

40/40

This essay is very strong in terms of own knowledge and the source use. Own knowledge is detailed, precise, accurate and focused. Additionally, the essay is well structured. The candidate has selected information from the sources to support and challenge the view expressed in the question, and gains a mark in Level 4 by weighing the evidence of the sources in paragraph 4 and in the conclusion.

Section 2: Conservative Governments, 1951–1964

Post-war consensus

In 1950, Labour won a second election victory. However, Attlee only gained a **Commons majority** of six, so in October 1951 he called another election, hoping to win a larger majority. Labour won a larger number of votes, but the **First Past the Post** system gave the Conservatives a majority of seats in the Commons.

Between 1951–1964, the Conservatives won three elections and Britain was governed by four Prime Ministers.

Year	Prime Minister
1951	Winston Churchill
1955	Anthony Eden
1957	Harold Macmillan
1963	Alec Douglas-Home

Election	Vote	Commons majority
1951	Conservative: 48.0% Labour: 48.8%	Conservative: 16
1955	Conservative: 49.7% Labour: 46.4%	Conservative: 60
1959	Conservative: 49.4% Labour: 43.8%	Conservative: 100

Butskellism

The new Conservative Government of 1951 continued many of the policies initiated by the Attlee Labour Government, including:

- a commitment to full employment through Keynesian economic management
- high levels of state-funded welfare
- a mixed economy.

The consensus between the leaders of the two main parties became known as 'Butskellism', a satirical reference to the similarity in the policies of Rab Butler, the Conservative Chancellor of the Exchequer, and Hugh Gaitskell, Labour's Shadow Chancellor.

Reasons for the consensus

- Although the Conservatives won a parliamentary majority in the 1951 election, Labour won more votes. Consequently, Conservative leaders recognised the election result was not a **mandate** for radical change.

- Labour's key policies were genuinely popular. The Conservatives realised that they risked losing the next election if they ended the welfare state or abandoned the commitment to full employment.

- **Keynesianism** seemed to be successfully generating economic growth.

- Important figures in the Conservative Government, such as Butler and Harold Macmillan, were ideologically committed to the welfare state and **full employment**.

Rab Butler

Butler was a Conservative MP and Cabinet Minister. During Churchill's wartime Government, Butler was responsible for the 1944 Education Act (see page 4). He described himself as a 'One Nation Conservative', that is, a Conservative who believed that the Government should pursue policies that served the whole nation rather than just the rich.

Butler's commitment to **One Nation Conservatism** was evident in his policy statements of the late 1940s. For example, the **Industrial Charter** of 1947 committed the Conservative Party to support many Labour policies including the introduction of the mixed economy and protection of the rights of workers.

During the Conservative Government of 1951–1955, Butler continued Labour's policies on welfare and full employment.

The limits of the consensus

The Conservatives left much of the Labour legacy untouched. However, **nationalisation** was the least popular aspect of Labour's achievements. The public refused to support the nationalisation of the sugar industry (see page 12). Additionally, because rail nationalisation had failed to improve services, many people were convinced that nationalisation could not solve the country's economic problems. Therefore, the Conservatives felt they could denationalise industries such as iron, steel and road haulage.

Support or challenge?

Below is a sample exam-style part (a) question which asks how far the sources agree with a specific statement. Below this are three sources which give information relevant to the question. Identify whether the sources support, mainly support, mainly challenge, or challenge the statement in the question and then give reasons for your answer.

Study Sources 1, 2 and 3. How far do Sources 1, 2 and 3 suggest that the economic policies of the Conservative and Labour Parties were similar in the years 1951–1955?

SOURCE 1

(From the Labour Party election manifesto, 1955)

Even the Tories have had to praise the nationalised industries for their high rate of investment and advances in technical efficiency.

Public ownership of the steel and road haulage industries is essential to the nation's needs and we shall re-nationalise them.

We shall bring sections of the chemical and machine tools industries into public ownership. Where necessary, we shall start new public enterprises.

SOURCE 2

(From the Conservative Party election manifesto, 1955)

The Conservative Party is strongly opposed to any further measure of nationalisation. The denationalised iron and steel industry is breaking production records month by month. Those sections of our economy that remain nationalised must be brought to a higher peak of efficiency.

The Labour Party still cling to the broken reed of nationalisation. Their policy is to multiply restraints; our policy is to multiply opportunities. Their policies would involve an increase in Government spending so huge that there could be no saving for purposes of investment.

SOURCE 3

'Dear old pals' cartoon by Vicky (Victor Weisz), Daily Mirror, 1954

DEAR OLD PALS . . .

Linking sources

Above are a sample exam-style part (a) question and the three sources referred to in the question. In one colour, draw links between the sources to show ways in which they agree about how far the economic policies of the Conservative and Labour Parties were similar in the years 1951–1955. In another colour, draw links between the sources to show ways in which they disagree.

Conservative domestic policy, 1951–1964

Conservative domestic policy mainly continued the high levels of state intervention initiated by the previous Labour Government. Broadly, the Conservatives achieved their goals of maintaining full employment, building large numbers of new houses and continuing the welfare state.

Full employment

Conservative leaders were committed to maintaining full employment. In 1951, there were 367,000 unemployed. When unemployment began to rise in 1952 the Government quickly responded with **public works schemes**, such as a **tidal barrage** across the River Severn, ensuring that levels of employment remained high. Between 1952 and 1955, unemployment figures never exceeded half a million, and in 1955 and 1956 there were never more than 300,000 unemployed.

Although unemployment increased again between 1958 and 1964, peaking at 878,000 in 1963, there was no return to the interwar mass unemployment.

Housing

The 1951 Conservative manifesto promised that a new Conservative Government would build 300,000 houses a year. Between 1952 and 1954, Harold Macmillan (the Housing Minister at that time) kept this promise. Following 1954, the pace slowed, but in total the Conservatives created 1.7 million new homes during 1952–1964.

The 1957 Rent Act limited government control of the rental market, allowing landlords greater freedom to set rents. It reflected the Conservative view that the free market, rather than the Government, was best for ensuring affordable housing.

Social policy

The Conservatives continued to support the NHS. Butler's first budget introduced charges of two shillings for every prescription. However, this was not a radical break with Labour policy as Hugh Gaitskell had introduced charges in Labour's 1951 budget. In 1953, the Government underlined its commitment to the NHS by accepting the findings of the Guillebaud Committee, which concluded that the NHS provided value for money.

Macmillan's Government built on this commitment. The Conservatives published a plan to build 90 new NHS hospitals, remodel 134 existing hospitals and improve a further 356 hospitals in 1962. This was the biggest expansion of the NHS since its creation.

The Conservatives continued to administer the model of education that the Butler Act had introduced (see page 4). However, government reports – for example, the 1959 Crowther Report and 1963 Newsom Report – criticised the **tripartite** system, arguing that it hindered social mobility. Consequently, the Government faced pressure to introduce a non-selective education model.

The Conservatives also increased the proportion of government spending devoted to welfare from 39.2 per cent in 1951 to 43 per cent in 1955.

Right-wing alternatives to consensus

A minority of Conservative MPs believed a more free market approach should replace consensus policies. Operation ROBOT was a free market policy advocated in 1952 by three senior ministers (including Butler). It proposed solving Britain's **balance of payment** difficulties by ending sterling's role as a **reserve currency**, allowing it to **float freely**. This would have opened the British economy to foreign markets, forcing more competition among British firms. Consequently, firms would have to cut jobs to reduce their costs, and Operation ROBOT would have ended full employment. Anthony Eden led the Cabinet majority in rejecting the plan. Right-wing Cabinet Ministers argued that the Government was sacrificing economic efficiency to preserve full employment.

Enoch Powell also criticised how **inflation** was allowed to rise during the late 1950s. He argued, unsuccessfully, that cuts in government spending were essential to stop inflation rising.

Complete the table

Use the information on the opposite page to add detail to the table below.

	Labour policy	Conservative policy	Degree of consensus
Employment			
Housing			
Health			
Education			
Welfare			

Explain the difference

The following sources give different accounts of the impact of the Conservative Government on employment in the period 1951–1963. List the ways in which the sources differ. Explain the differences between the sources using the provenance of the sources alone. The provenance appears at the top of the source in brackets.

SOURCE 1

(From Michael Lynch, Britain 1945–2007, *published 2008)*

Although the Conservatives willingly inherited the Labour Party's commitment to full employment as a basic economic aim, achieving this proved much more difficult. The lowest annual figure for joblessness was well over a quarter of a million in the mid-1950s, rose rapidly in the late 1950s, and, after falling in the early 1960s, reached an embarrassingly high figure in Macmillan's final year in government. The persistence of high unemployment cast doubt on just how realistic it was to claim that the people had 'never had it so good'.

SOURCE 2

(From the Conservative Party election manifesto, 1959)

The British economy is sounder today than at any time since the First World War. We have now stabilised the cost of living while maintaining full employment. We have shown that Conservative freedom works. Life is better with the Conservatives.

The achievements of economic management, 1951–1964

Revised

Keynesianism

Between 1951 and 1964, Conservative Chancellors used **fiscal policy** and **monetary policy** to manage the economy according to Keynesianism.

- In 1954, Butler cut income tax by 6d and reduced interest rates.

- Butler's 1954 measures increased inflation. He then increased interest rates and **indirect taxes** to try to bring inflation down.

- The Conservatives cut income tax again in 1956 and 1959, leading to a boom in 1959 and 1960.

- The boom led to a rise in inflation. The Government tried to combat inflation by raising interest rates and increasing indirect taxes. However, this caused unemployment to rise.

- The Conservatives cut income tax again in 1963. However, rather than stimulating growth, this led to higher demands for imports which caused a **balance of payments deficit**.

Critics described Conservative attempts to manage the economy as 'stop-go economics': they led to short periods of rapid growth, followed by economic problems which necessitated an economic slowdown.

Affluence

Most types of rationing, including the rationing of sweets and sugar, came to an end in 1953. Austerity was soon replaced with an affluent consumer society. For example, between 1951 and 1964, the number of privately owned cars rose from 2.5 million to 8 million. Equally, by 1960, over 80 per cent of British people owned a radio, over 70 per cent owned a vacuum cleaner, and around 50 per cent owned a washing machine.

The feeling of new wealth was captured in Macmillan's famous statement that 'most of our people have never had it so good'.

How widespread was affluence under the Conservatives?

In spite of the new affluence there were signs that the good times were not equally shared. One indication of this was the high amount of goods bought on credit. For example, blue collar families tended to buy consumer goods on credit, whereas white collar families bought consumer goods from savings. A contemporary report on consumer rights showed that between 1952 and 1962, the number of repossessions of goods bought on credit doubled.

The 1957 independent study *Young Mothers at Work* indicated that working-class women had been left out of the affluent society. The study showed that married women were often forced to work because the extra income was necessary to avoid living in poverty. Only 2 per cent of the working women interviewed spent any of their income on luxuries.

Critics on the Left

Some on the Left were critical of the new consumerism. J.K. Galbraith's book *The Affluent Society* (1958), which focused on the USA, was widely read in Britain. He argued that western economies needed to be rebalanced and to move away from consumer spending towards public spending. He recommended raising indirect taxes to curb consumer spending and using the proceeds to fund public services.

Bevan made a similar point in a speech at the 1959 Labour Party Conference, arguing that 'this so-called affluent society is an ugly society … in which priorities have all gone wrong'.

Antony Crosland's book *The Future of Socialism* (1956) was more positive about rising living standards. However, he was concerned that the desire for more and more consumer goods would lead to selfishness and therefore, in the long run, declining support for public services.

Support or challenge?

Below is a sample exam-style part (b) question which asks you how far the sources agree with a specific statement. Below this are three sources which give information relevant to the question. Identify whether the sources support, mainly support, mainly challenge, or challenge the statement in the question and then give reasons for your answer.

Use Sources 1, 2 and 3 and your own knowledge. Do you agree with the view that Britain enjoyed unprecedented prosperity during the 1950s?

SOURCE 1

(From a speech by Harold Macmillan, 20 July 1957)

You will see a state of prosperity such as we have never had in my lifetime – nor indeed in the history of this country. Indeed let us be frank about it – most of our people have never had it so good. Go around the country, go to the industrial towns, go to the farms and you will see a state of prosperity such as we have never had in my lifetime – nor indeed in the history of this country.

> This source <u>supports</u> / <u>mainly supports</u> / <u>mainly challenges</u> / challenges the view that living standards were high in the 1950s because
>
> _____
>
> _____

SOURCE 2

(From Steven Fielding, The Labour Governments 1964–71: Volume 1, *published 2008)*

On the eve of the 1960s, the working class was richer than ever before. Between the mid-1950s and mid-1960s, a male worker's average income rose by a third in real terms; the proportion of households owning fridges went from one in ten to one in three; and those with a television set increased from two-fifths to two-thirds. In this context, it was not unreasonable for the Conservative Prime Minister, Harold Macmillan, to declare that 'most of our people have never had it so good'.

> This source <u>supports</u> / <u>mainly supports</u> / <u>mainly challenges</u> / challenges the view that living standards were high in the 1950s because
>
> _____
>
> _____

SOURCE 3

(From Gordon Marshall, Poverty in an Affluent Society, *published 2002)*

Throughout the so-called years of affluence a small group of commentators consistently maintained that the problem of poverty was still widespread. These commentators identified a number of minority groups, including the old, the widowed, the sick and the disabled, who were unable to participate in the expanding economy. Collectively these groups probably numbered some 7 million people.

> This source <u>supports</u> / <u>mainly supports</u> / <u>mainly challenges</u> / <u>challenges</u> the view that living standards were high in the 1950s because
>
> _____
>
> _____

Add own knowledge

Above are a sample part (b) question and the three sources referred to in the question. In one colour, draw links between the sources to show ways in which they agree about living standards in the 1950s. In another colour, draw links between the sources to show ways in which they disagree. Around the edge of the sources, write relevant own knowledge. Again, draw links to show the ways in which this agrees and disagrees with the sources.

Economic problems and corporatism, 1959–1964

Revised

Relative economic decline

By the end of the 1950s, British politicians were concerned about Britain's relative economic decline (RED). After 1950, Japan, West Germany, France and the USA were growing faster than Britain. Therefore, by comparison, Britain was declining.

Country	Rate of growth, 1950–1973
Japan	9.4%
West Germany	6%
France	5%
USA	3.7%
Britain	3%

Leading figures in both the Labour and Conservative Parties were convinced that Britain needed to achieve higher growth rates to maintain its position as a major economic power.

Conservative corporatism

Macmillan believed that the solution to Britain's RED was greater state intervention. Following the example of the French Government, Macmillan decided to try **corporatism**, an approach whereby the Government worked together with the unions and employers to increase growth. For Macmillan, corporatism was a new version of traditional One Nation Conservatism as it brought together the two sides of industry for the good of the whole nation. Macmillan hoped that a corporatist approach would allow British economic growth to reach 4 per cent a year.

Macmillan's two new corporatist institutions were the National Economic Development Council and the National Economic Development Office (together, known as 'Neddy') established in 1962, and the National Incomes Commission ('Nicky'), also set up in 1962.

National Economic Development Council and Office ('Neddy')

Essentially, 'Neddy' brought employers, unions and the Government together in a tripartite structure. It was designed as a forum in which employers and workers could discuss common goals and make voluntary agreements to help industry grow. Macmillan hoped that better communication between management and workers, and government help, would lead to economic efficiency and growth. 'Neddy' had the support of the **Federation of British Industry** and the **Trades Union Congress (TUC)**, but its powers were limited and its role was purely advisory. Therefore it could not force either unions or employers to accept its proposals.

National Incomes Commission ('Nicky')

For some years the Conservative Government had been seeking voluntary agreements to limit pay increases. For example, in 1961 the Government advised that pay should increase by no more than 2.5 per cent. Macmillan also introduced a '**pay-pause**' for all **public sector workers**, thinking that **wage restraint** would halt growing inflation. In 1962, he went further, establishing 'Nicky', a panel of independent experts who advised the Government on appropriate wage rates to help persuade unions and employers to stick to government pay recommendations. Significantly, 'Nicky', like 'Neddy', had a purely advisory role and could not force unions or management to change their pay deals.

Critics of Conservative corporatism

Left-wing critics argued that Macmillan's corporatism did not go far enough. They argued that the Government should pass laws forbidding wage increases that exceeded 'Nicky's' recommendations.

Right-wing critics argued that Macmillan's approach was counterproductive. Powell, for example, argued that less government intervention was the solution to RED. He argued that the Government should control inflation by cutting government spending and abandoning its commitment to full employment. Powell believed that these measures would make British industry more competitive.

Explain the difference

Sources 1 and 2 give different accounts of the significance of the creation of the National Economic Development Council. List the ways in which the sources differ. Explain the differences between the sources using the provenance of the sources alone. The provenance appears at the top of the source in brackets.

SOURCE 1

(From a speech by Jo Grimond, leader of the Liberal Party, 10 April 1962)

The tasks of the [National Economic Development] Council are, first, the examination of economic performance; secondly, the consideration of obstacles to growth; and, thirdly, seeking agreement about ways of improving economic performance. There is no indication that the Government will do anything themselves. Apparently, they are to sit by and leave it to the National Economic Development Council.

I do not believe that that is what the nation expected from the Government when it heard of this Council, and I do not believe that this Council is a suitable instrument for tackling these tasks, which are the tasks of the Government and which can be tackled by no one else.

SOURCE 2

(From a speech by Harold Macmillan at the 1962 Conservative Party Conference)

During the last year, the Government have taken two important forward steps in planning – 'Nicky', the National Incomes Commission, to ensure that rates of reward are both fair and in step with what we produce; and 'Neddy', the National Economic Development Council, to help us produce more, and produce more efficiently, by keeping our plans in line with our resources and by removing obstacles to growth.

SOURCE 3

(From Hans Daalder, Cabinet Reform in Britain, *published 1963. Daalder was Professor of Politics at Leiden University in the Netherlands)*

Both 'Nicky' and 'Neddy' lack teeth. For all the new appeal of 'planning', the Government is not prepared to adopt economic controls. But economic growth cannot be produced solely by monthly meetings of leading industrial representatives, no matter how persuasive they may be. It demands appropriate action by the Government.

Eliminate irrelevance

Below is a sample exam-style part (a) question that refers to Sources 1, 2 and 3. There is also a paragraph written in answer to this question. Read the paragraph and identify parts of the paragraph that are not directly relevant to the question. Draw a line through the information that is irrelevant and justify your deletions in the margin.

Study Sources 1, 2 and 3.

How far do Sources 1 and 3 challenge the view presented in Source 2 that the creation of the National Economic Development Council was an 'important forward step'?

To an extent, Sources 1 and 3 agree with Source 2 that the creation of the National Economic Development Council was an 'important forward step'. This Council was created in 1962, and, together with the National Economic Development Office, was known as 'Neddy'. Source 1 agrees with Source 2 that the Council had important responsibilities. Source 2 states that the Council must ensure that Britain 'produce[s] more efficiently' and, similarly, Source 1 states that the Council must consider 'ways of improving economic performance'. The Council was set up to encourage workers and employers to discuss the ways in which they could work together to help the economy to grow. In addition, Source 2 states that the Council will be 'removing obstacles to growth', and Source 1 agrees, stating that the Council will consider 'obstacles to growth'. Furthermore, Source 3 agrees with Source 2 about the nature of this 'important forward step': Source 2 states that it is an 'important forward step in planning', and Source 3 (from Hans Daalder's book 'Cabinet Reform in Britain', published in 1963) links the creation of the Council to 'the new appeal of "planning"'. In this way, Source 1 and 3 agree with Source 2 that the Council was an 'important forward step' in planning for economic growth.

'Supermac': The role of Harold Macmillan

In 1958, the *Evening Standard* published a cartoon of Macmillan dressed as Superman. 'Supermac' was intended to poke fun, but the nickname soon became a positive part of his image, referring to the economic success associated with his Government in the late 1950s.

Background and beliefs

Macmillan was born into a wealthy family. In 1924, he was elected as Conservative MP for Stockton-on-Tees, a largely working-class area that was hit hard by the depression. He then became an advocate of government intervention to help the poor.

Macmillan as Prime Minister

The Suez Crisis (1956)

Anthony Eden, Conservative Prime Minister from 1955 to 1957, had authorised an invasion of Egypt to regain control of the Suez Canal. The Canal was a profitable trade route which used to belong to British and French companies until the Egyptian Government nationalised it in 1956. Eden publicly claimed the invasion was a peace-keeping exercise, but in reality he wanted to retake the Canal. The USA, which was trying to foster a better relationship with the Egyptian Government, refused to authorise loans to Britain and pressured them to withdraw. This meant that Britain could not import vital goods and it temporarily crippled the British economy. Britain was forced to end the conflict. Eden resigned for misleading the public and taking the country into an unsuccessful war.

Consensus Prime Minister

Macmillan played a key role in sustaining the consensus. He did so for several reasons.

- He was committed to full employment due to his experience of the depression. Consequently, while Butler and Eden were willing to allow unemployment to rise (so they could control inflation), Macmillan always prioritised full employment over **deflationary policies**.

- He was committed to Keynesianism. His book *The Middle Way* (1938) argued that Britain should avoid socialism, whereby the Government controlled the economy, and free market capitalism, whereby the Government played a minor economic role. Rather, the Government should manage the economy and ensure high levels of employment, set a minimum wage and guarantee benefits for the poor.

- He was highly pragmatic, and therefore continued policies which he believed would lead to economic growth.

Macmillan's endorsement of consensus politics was evident in his 1959 election manifesto, which was the most moderate Conservative manifesto of the period.

Commitment to full employment

Macmillan's loyalty to full employment was so great that he neglected other economic priorities. Consequently, inflation, which had averaged 3.6 per cent in the 1950s, grew to 5.5 per cent in the early 1960s. Equally, the balance of payments situation worsened from a surplus of £345 million in 1958 to a deficit of £258 million in 1960.

Unflappable Mac

Macmillan was often described as 'unflappable', a calm leader who could take anything in his stride. This was very appealing to voters in the late 1950s when the British economy appeared to be doing well. However, in the early 1960s, when economic problems returned (see page 30), his relaxed style and his privileged background implied that he was out of touch.

Managing decline

Whereas Churchill and Eden wanted to maintain the British Empire, Macmillan recognised that Britain could no longer play a major world role. Therefore, he emphasised international co-operation with the USA and advocated entry to the **European Economic Community (EEC)**.

Doing reliability well **a**

Below are a series of definitions listing common reasons why sources are either reliable or unreliable, and two sources. Under each source, explain why the source is either reliable or unreliable for the purpose stated, justifying your answer by referring to the following definitions.

- **Vested interest**: the source is written so that the writer can protect their power or their financial interests.
- **Second-hand report:** the writer of the source is not an eyewitness, but is relying on someone else's account.
- **Expertise**: the source is written on a subject on which the author (for example, a historian) is an expert.
- **Political bias**: the source is written by a politician and it reflects their political views.
- **Reputation**: the source is written to protect the writer's reputation.

SOURCE 1

(From a speech by Hugh Gaitskell, leader of the Labour Party, 19 November 1957)

The Prime Minister, of course, is as usual rude and arrogant. Neither his answer nor his manner addresses the issue here. I would ask him again, since a Royal Commission is investigating the whole question of doctors' and dentists' payment, whether he is prepared to give an assurance that the recommendations of such a Royal Commission will be considered on their merits by the Government and will not be rejected in the same manner as previous health service issues?

The source is <u>reliable / fairly reliable / fairly unreliable / unreliable</u> as evidence of the character of Harold Macmillan because

_____

_____

SOURCE 2

(From the recollections of Margaret Warnock, a housewife in Glasgow in 1959)

Harold Macmillan was not very impressive as Prime Minister. He did not keep his promises. He did not live up to my expectations. However, when I read interviews with him, he seemed a nice fellow, charming and well-meaning. He came across well in those interviews.

The source is <u>reliable / fairly reliable / fairly unreliable / unreliable</u> as evidence of the character of Harold Macmillan because

_____

_____

 ## Write the question **a**

The sources on this page relate to the character of Harold Macmillan. Write an exam-style part (a) question using the sources.

Study Sources 1, 2 and 3. How far do the sources agree that ...

_____

_____

SOURCE 3

(From Lord Kilmuir, Political Adventure: the Memoirs of the Earl of Kilmuir, *published 1964. Lord Kilmuir was Lord Chancellor from 1954 until 1962)*

The Labour Party seriously underrated Macmillan from the outset, but before long they began to become singularly uneasy. His calm confidence, his courtesy and sharpness in debate, his quick-wittedness under pressure, and, above all, his superb professionalism, unnerved and disconcerted his opponents until he secured a quite astonishing psychological superiority in the commons.

Thirteen wasted years? Why Labour won in 1964

Macmillan's Government experienced several problems in the early 1960s and, consequently, Macmillan resigned in 1963. Sir Alec Douglas-Home, Macmillan's replacement, did not restore public confidence in the Conservatives. Their failings and Labour's increasing appeal led to a Labour victory in 1964.

Growing problems, 1960–1963

Economic problems

By 1963, Britain was facing renewed economic problems.

- Unemployment was 878,000.
- Unions refused to adopt the pay restraint advised by Nicky.
- Average economic growth shrank to 2 per cent a year.
- Balance of payments problems meant that Britain was forced to borrow £714 million from the **International Monetary Fund (IMF)** to support the value of the pound.

The Government also adopted plans to reduce the size of the British rail network. The **Beeching Report** caused 33 per cent of rail routes to close in an attempt to save money.

Security scandals

The Macmillan Government was rocked by three security scandals.

- In October 1962, William Vassall, a civil servant with access to naval secrets, was found guilty of passing secrets to Russia.
- In January 1963, Kim Philby, head of MI6, the Secret Intelligence Service, defected to Russia.
- In June 1963, John Profumo, the Government's Secretary of State for War, confessed to an affair with showgirl Christine Keeler, who was also having an affair with Captain Yevgeni Ivanov, a Russian diplomat and spy. The Profumo Affair, as it came to be called, was particularly damaging because Profumo publicly denied sleeping with Keeler. This led many to question the honesty of the Government.

Policy failure

The clearest signs of the Government's failure were the EEC's rejection of Macmillan and the unforeseen consequences of the 1957 Rent Act.

Following the Suez Crisis (see page 28), Macmillan argued that Britain needed to work more closely with other European nations. During 1962–1963, he attempted to negotiate Britain's entry to the EEC, but his negotiations failed because Britain's entry was vetoed by French President Charles De Gaulle.

The Conservatives introduced the Rent Act in 1957. This led to landlords charging high rents for dilapidated accommodation. The shortage of accommodation meant that tenants had no choice but to pay these high rents. By the early 1960s, the problem, known as Rachmanism, was widespread.

Image problems

In the early 1960s, Macmillan was the focus of satirical attacks. Comedians, particularly on the BBC TV show *That Was The Week That Was*, portrayed him as upper class, dithering and out of touch. Macmillan's attempt to fight back backfired. He allowed the BBC to film him during his free time, shooting grouse, which only emphasised his privileged lifestyle.

Douglas-Home, older and more privileged, followed Macmillan as Prime Minister but his performance on television was so bad that his critics compared him to a ventriloquist's dummy. Labour capitalised on Conservative image problems with the slogan 'thirteen wasted years'.

Labour's alternative

Harold Wilson, who became Labour leader in 1963, was younger and more dynamic than Macmillan or Douglas-Home. Educated at a grammar school rather than a public school, and with a northern accent, he came across as 'classless', unlike his Conservative rivals who were obviously from rich backgrounds. Wilson could also present himself as an expert economist as he had an economics degree from Oxford University. Therefore, in many ways, Wilson seemed the perfect alternative to the old-fashioned, upper-class Conservative leaders.

Develop the detail

(a)

Below are a sample exam-style part (b) question and a paragraph written in answer to this question. The question refers to the sources on this page. The paragraph contains a limited amount of detail. Annotate the paragraph to add additional detail to the answer.

Use Sources 1, 2 and 3 and your own knowledge. Do you agree with the view that the Labour victory in the general election of 1964 was due to 'the collapse of Conservative strength' (Source 2)?

Although Source 2 argues that the Labour victory in the general election of 1964 was due to 'the collapse of Conservative strength', there is evidence in the sources to challenge this view. Sources 1 and 3 both argue that the result was due to the strengths of the Labour Party rather than the weaknesses of the Conservatives. Source 1 highlights strengths of leadership, stating that 'Wilson's poll ratings remained way ahead of Home's'. Harold Wilson was younger and more dynamic than his Conservative rival, Sir Alec Douglas-Home. As a result, Wilson appealed to a wide section of British society. In addition, the sources draw attention to the strengths of Labour policy. Source 1 argues that 'Labour's insistent talk of "thirteen wasted years" of Tory Government succeeded in catching a mood for change'. The Labour Party election campaign was effective at exploiting the weaknesses of the Tories. For example, Labour suggested that little economic progress had been made under the Conservative Government. Source 3 supports the argument that it was Labour policy that attracted voters to the party. Wilson states that 'we are here because millions of our fellow countrymen ... look to us to provide a strong Britain, a healthy Britain, and to create and maintain a new and fair order of society'. In this way, the Labour victory in the general election of 1964 was partly due to strengths of leadership and policy on the part of the Labour Party.

SOURCE 1

(From Steven Fielding, The Labour Governments 1964–71: Volume 1, *published 2008)*

The 1964 result was due more to the collapse of Conservative strength rather than any Labour recovery. The government had been unable to restore its authority after the Profumo scandal and Macmillan's failure to take Britain into the EEC. Moreover, it was increasingly apparent that the relative performance of the British economy was unimpressive, as other countries were beginning to catch up.

SOURCE 2

(From a speech by Harold Wilson to the Labour Party Conference, 1965. The speech followed Labour's election to government)

We are here because of the countless thousands of our supporters, motivated not by thought of personal advantage but by devotion to a great ideal: we are here because of millions of our fellow countrymen who look to us to provide a strong Britain, a healthy Britain, and to create and maintain a new and fair order of society.

SOURCE 3

(From Peter Clarke, Hope and Glory, *published 1996)*

Labour's insistent talk of 'thirteen wasted years' of Tory government succeeded in catching a mood for change. Wilson's poll ratings remained way ahead of Home's ... yet Home's performance should not be criticised. After all, he inherited a demoralised party [and] to many people's surprise, the general election in October 1964 turned out to be a close-run thing.

Recommended reading

Below is a list of suggested further reading on this topic.
- *Britain 1945–2007*, pages 36–72, Michael Lynch (2008)
- *MacMillan*, pages 94–113, Francis Beckett (2006)
- *Leading Labour: From Keir Hardie to Tony Blair*, pages 121–28, Kevin Jeffreys (1999)

Section 2: Exam focus

On pages 33–35 are sample answers to the exam-style questions on this page. Read the answers and the examiner comments around them.

a) Study Sources 1, 2 and 3.

How far do the sources agree on the similarities between Labour and the Conservatives in the period 1951–1959? Explain your answer using the evidence of Sources 1, 2 and 3. (20 marks)

b) Use Sources 4, 5 and 6 and your own knowledge.

Do you agree with the view that in terms of the economy, the Conservative Government of 1951–1964 was responsible for 'thirteen wasted years'? Explain your answer using Sources 4, 5 and 6 and your own knowledge. (40 marks)

SOURCE 1

(From 'Mr Butskell's Dilemma', The Economist, 13 February 1954)

Mr Butskell is already a well-known figure in dinner table conversations in both Westminster and Whitehall. He is a mix of the present Chancellor and the previous one. Whenever there are radicals within the Conservative Party who call for a little more unemployment to teach the unions a lesson – Mr Butskell speaks up for moderation from the government side of the Commons. When there is a clamour for greater irresponsibility from the Labour benches, the Labour Mr Butskell speaks up for moderation.

SOURCE 2

(From The Times, 24 January 1953)

Herbert Morrison MP gave an outline of the aim of Labour Party policy in a lecture last night. 'Of course, the Labour Party will renationalise iron and steel as well as road transportation, if this silly Government succeed in messing up the industry by its denationalisation Bill,' he said. However, he emphasised that it was not going to be as easy as it had been in 1945 to produce a definite list of industries to be nationalised.

SOURCE 3

(From a speech by Hugh Gaitskell at the Labour Party Conference, November 1959)

The Conservatives tell us that we have succeeded so well in reforming capitalism that our best bet is to accept it completely. The Labour Party points out rightly how much remains to be done. Indeed, the improvements in the Welfare State are urgently needed. Buses are overcrowded and slow, not because nationalised industries are inefficient, but because of the state of London traffic which the Tory Government has neglected all these years.

Turning to nationalisation, we regard public ownership as a means to full employment, greater equality and higher productivity. But we do not aim to nationalise every private firm.

SOURCE 4

(From David Dutton, British Politics since 1945, published 1997)

The Conservative Party rapidly lost its political momentum from 1961 onwards. The government and the Prime Minister lost their reputation for competence, which had been so important in winning elections in the 1950s. They proved unable to achieve sustained economic growth without dangerously overheating the economy. After an inflationary budget in 1961 the Chancellor was obliged to bring in a deflationary 'pay pause'. Labour derided the government's economic management as 'stop-go'.

SOURCE 5

(From the Labour Party election manifesto, 1964)

The Labour Party offers a 'New Britain', reversing the decline of the thirteen wasted years, affording a new opportunity to equal, and if possible surpass, the progress of other western nations. Tory Britain has moved sideways, backwards but seldom forward.

SOURCE 6

(From Stephen J. Lee, Aspects of British Political History: 1914–1995, published 1996)

The Conservative governments, 1951–64, certainly presided over a major improvement in living standards. Wages rose by 72 per cent, prices by only 45 per cent. Car ownership increased by 500 per cent, and television ownership from 4 per cent of the population to 91 per cent. Prosperity was enhanced by tax cuts. Conservatives also delivered improvements in living conditions. In the early years they met their building target of 300,000 new homes a year. However, in comparative terms Britain's growth-rate was unimpressive: Germany's was four times as rapid, Japan's ten times.

a) Study Sources 1, 2 and 3.

How far do the sources agree on the similarities between Labour and the Conservatives in the period 1951–1959? Explain your answer using the evidence of Sources 1, 2 and 3. (20 marks)

The sources suggest that there was a large amount of consensus between the leadership of both parties. However, Source 1 indicates that there was less consensus on the back benches, Source 2 shows that some areas were not part of the consensus and Source 3 shows that while there was consensus on policy, there was less consensus on values.

The introduction clearly answers the question and summarises the view of each of the sources.

All three sources suggest that there was a large degree of consensus between the Conservatives and Labour in the years 1951–1959. Source 1 illustrates this with the satirical character 'Mr Butskell ... a mix of the present Chancellor and the previous one', a moderate who resists extreme policies from left and right. Source 2 also shows a degree of moderation. Herbert Morrison argues that while the Labour Party is still committed to nationalisation 'he emphasised that it was not going to be as easy as it had been in 1945 to produce a definite list of industries to be nationalised'. In context, Morrison's statement was addressed to Party members who wanted more nationalisation. In this way, he urged moderation. In Source 3, Gaitskell also emphasised that Labour would not 'nationalise every firm'. Again, Source 3 is a statement to the Labour Party outside Parliament, and therefore Gaitskell is using the speech to persuade his party of the need for moderation. In calling for moderation, Gaitskell plays exactly the role in Source 3 that Butskell plays in Source 1. In this way, Sources 1, 2 and 3 all indicate that there was great consensus because key leaders of the main parties are all advocating moderation.

This paragraph immediately highlights a similarity between all three sources, and therefore begins the essay with clear comparison.

However, the consensus was not complete. Sources 1, 2 and 3 show that there were disagreements over nationalisation. Source 1 indicates that behind the moderate leadership there are radicals on the back benches who are calling for 'more unemployment' or 'greater irresponsibility'. Sources 2 and 3 both show Labour was critical of Conservative denationalisation. Source 3 criticises the 'state of London traffic which the Tory Government has neglected all these years', again attacking the Conservative's denationalisation of the transport industry. Sources 2 and 3 also show that the Labour Party is more committed to nationalisation than the Conservatives. In Source 2, Morrison commits the Labour Party to 'renationalise iron and steel', a clear criticism of Conservative policy. Similarly, Gaitskell, in Source 3, sets out Labour's commitment to nationalisation as 'we regard public ownership as a means to full employment, greater equality and higher productivity'. Finally, Gaitskell, Labour's leader in 1959, sets out a serious difference with the Conservatives, arguing that he does not accept their argument that they have succeeded 'in reforming capitalism'. Clearly, the issue of nationalisation divided the parties reflecting deeper concerns, such as how far capitalism had been reformed.

In this paragraph the candidate shows that they are aware of the context of Source 2 and Source 3, and this information is used to draw a conclusion about how the sources are similar.

Here, the candidate provides a counter-argument, showing the limits to consensus.

The paragraph ends with a summary of the evidence in the paragraph.

In conclusion, the three sources, which refer to Butler, Gaitskell and Morrison, show that there was a great deal of consensus among the leadership of the two main parties. However, Sources 2 and 3 in particular argue that others in the parties were more radical, and that there were genuine differences over nationalisation.

The conclusion is consistent with the introduction.

20/20

This essay gets a mark in Level 4 because it contains a detailed comparison of the sources, with a strong focus on the question. The mark is at the top of Level 4 because the essay places the evidence of the sources in their historical context, and uses this to provide a sophisticated answer to the question. In addition, there is sustained focus on how far the sources agree and disagree.

b) Use Sources 4, 5 and 6 and your own knowledge.

Do you agree with the view that in terms of the economy, the Conservative Government of 1951–1964 was responsible for 'thirteen wasted years'? Explain your answer using Sources 4, 5 and 6 and your own knowledge. (40 marks)

During the election campaign of 1964 Labour argued that the Conservatives were responsible for 'thirteen wasted years'. This is certainly the message of Source 5, an extract from the Labour manifesto of 1964. However, as Source 6 argues, the Conservative Governments of 1951–1964 could claim credit for a major increase in the standard of living. Nonetheless, as Source 4 argues, there were ongoing problems with Conservative economic policy, and, as Source 6 points out, compared to other countries they did waste thirteen years.

Source 5 clearly indicates that the Conservative Governments from 1951 to 1964 wasted thirteen years. It argues, 'Tory Britain has moved sideways, backwards but seldom forward'. The source focuses on Britain's relative economic decline, implying that the Conservatives had failed to equal or 'surpass, the progress of other western nations'. This accusation is true. In the late 1950s, it became clear that the economies of other industrial nations were growing much faster than that of Britain. For example, France was growing at 5 per cent, West Germany was growing at 6 per cent and Japan was growing at 9.4 per cent, while Britain's economy was only achieving a 3 per cent growth rate each year. Therefore, Source 6 is correct to argue that 'in comparative terms Britain's growth-rate was unimpressive'. The Conservatives acknowledged this problem in the early 1960s and set up the National Economic Development Council, the National Economic Development Office ('Neddy') and the National Incomes Commission ('Nicky') in 1962 to try to boost growth. However, in the early 1960s economic problems got worse. Growth shrank to 2 per cent a year and unemployment reached a post-war high at 878,000. Clearly, the Conservatives were responsible for wasting thirteen years because they failed to stop Britain's relative economic decline.

However, Source 6 argues that the 'Conservative governments, 1951–64, certainly presided over a major improvement in living standards'. It supports this with examples such as, incomes rising 'by 72 per cent, prices by only 45 per cent' and the wider availability of consumer goods such as televisions and cars. Living standards were supported by a continued commitment to high levels of welfare spending. For example, under Macmillan, the Conservatives built 90 new NHS hospitals and upgraded 134 existing hospitals. Additionally, at times of economic difficulty they invested in public works schemes, such as the 1952 River Severn tidal barrage, to maintain full employment. Finally, Source 6 points to Conservative successes in house building stating that, 'in the early years they met their building target of 300,000 new homes a year'. Indeed, between 1952 and 1964 the Conservatives succeeded in building '1.7 million new homes'. In this way, it is clear that the Conservatives had significant economic successes because the standard of living improved in terms of wages, the health service and housing.

The introduction uses all three sources and shows a good understanding of the period by referring to the origins of the phrase 'thirteen wasted years'.

This paragraph begins with the argument of Source 5.

In addition, the paragraph builds on Source 5's argument with detailed own knowledge, which is integrated well with the sources.

The own knowledge presented in this paragraph is extremely detailed, as the candidate uses specific figures and accurate dates.

Nonetheless, Source 4 argues that the Conservatives struggled to 'achieve sustained economic growth'. Indeed, as Source 4 argues, Labour accused the Conservatives of having a 'stop-go' policy. For example, Rab Butler's 1954 income tax cut led to an increase in inflation. Therefore, Butler was forced to increase indirect taxes to try to bring inflation down. Also, income tax cuts in 1956 and 1959 led to a boom in 1959 and 1960, again increasing inflation. Again the Government increased indirect taxes to try to reduce inflation. As Source 4 argues, the Conservatives 'rapidly lost its political momentum from 1961 onwards'. Their attempts to revive the economy failed. The Trades Union Congress refused to adopt the 'pay-pause' that 'Nicky' recommended. Finally, more tax cuts in 1963 led to a huge balance of payments deficit. By 1963, balance of payments problems were so bad that Britain was forced to borrow £714 million from the IMF to avoid devaluation. Overall, Conservative economic policy from 1951 to 1964 was responsible for thirteen wasted years because over the whole period the Government was never able to achieve sustained economic growth.

In conclusion, the Conservative Government of 1951–1964 was responsible for 'thirteen wasted years' in terms of the economy. Sources 5 and 6 show that under the Conservatives Britain experienced relative economic decline. Additionally, Source 4 shows that in spite of the rise in living standards mentioned in Source 6, the Conservatives only ever achieved 'stop-go' growth rather than economic expansion.

> Here, the candidate weighs the argument presented in Source 4 by using extensive own knowledge.

> The conclusion uses all three sources to reach an overall judgement that reflects the argument of the essay.

34/40

This essay is strong in terms of own knowledge and the use of the sources. Own knowledge is detailed, precise, accurate and focused. Additionally, the essay is extremely well structured. The candidate has selected information from the sources to support and challenge the view expressed in the question, and gains a mark in Level 4 by weighing the evidence of the sources in paragraph 2 and in the conclusion. Nonetheless, the essay does not get a mark at the top of Level 4 as the range of factors discussed is not extensive.

Extend the range

This exam focus Part (b) essay would achieve a higher mark if it discussed a more extensive range of factors. Use the sources and your own knowledge to write an additional paragraph for this essay.

Section 3: Consensus under pressure: Labour and Conservative Governments, 1964–1979

Labour Government, 1964–1970: Economic policy

The 1964 election gave Labour a small parliamentary majority. Harold Wilson called an election in 1966 to gain a larger majority. His gamble paid off and Labour gained a majority of almost 100.

Economic policy

The Wilson Government had three key economic goals:

- to increase growth – it aimed to achieve an annual rate of growth of 4 per cent
- to achieve a **balance of payments** surplus
- to avoid devaluing the pound.

Wilson attempted to achieve these goals through economic planning and **corporatism**.

Economic planning

In 1964, Wilson set up the Department for Economic Affairs (DEA). The DEA was tasked with creating and overseeing a National Plan, published in September 1965. However, this plan was based on highly optimistic assumptions and therefore had to be abandoned in July 1966.

Corporatism

In 1965, Wilson established the National Board for Prices and Incomes (NBPI) to extend corporatism. This attempted to bring the Government, industry and the unions together to help regulate the economy. Wilson hoped that **wage restraint** would reduce purchasing power and thus end the **balance of payments deficit** by decreasing demand.

Initially the NBPI recommended the rates by which wages should increase, and the prices of key products such as bread, sugar and soap. Over time the Government developed an **Incomes Policy**.

- From 1965 to 1966, the NBPI's recommendations on prices and incomes were voluntary. However, the Government publicly criticised companies that ignored its recommendations.
- The Prices and Incomes Act (1966) enforced a six-month wage freeze from July 1966.

- The Prices and Incomes Act (1967) allowed small wage increases in companies that increased **productivity**.

Finally, Wilson expanded the role of 'Neddy' (see page 26), creating 21 **'Little Neddies'** to oversee regional investment and development.

Industrial policy

Labour passed Acts which **nationalised** parts of British Industry.

- The Iron and Steel Act (1967) renationalised the iron and steel industries.
- The Transport Act (1968) created national bus and freight corporations.

In addition, in 1966, the Government set up the Industrial Reorganisation Corporation (IRC), which was designed to promote industrial efficiency by granting loans and organising mergers. For example, in 1968 the IRC organised the merger of five Scottish shipyards, granting the new company, Upper Clyde Shipbuilders, a loan of £20 million. The IRC loaned £103 million in total to British business between 1966 and 1970.

Devaluation

Despite Wilson's policies, the Government was unable to solve Britain's balance of payments problems. The **Arab-Israeli War** restricted the availability of oil and pushed the price up. Consequently, Britain's balance of payments deficit increased significantly. The Government was finally forced to devalue the pound. On 18 November 1967, the value of sterling dropped from £1:$2.80 to £1:$2.40. Devaluation was a huge embarrassment for the Government, leading to the resignation of James Callaghan, the Chancellor.

Labour's economic record

Evidence of success	Evidence of failure
• In 1968, British **GDP** grew by 4.1%. • By 1969, Britain had a balance of payments surplus of £445 million.	• The pound was devalued in 1967. • The National Plan was abandoned in July 1966. • In 1969, British GDP grew by 1.9%.

Spot the mistake

Below are a sample exam-style part (b) question and a paragraph written in answer to this question. Why does this paragraph not get into Level 4 for AO1? Once you have identified the mistake, rewrite the paragraph so that it displays the qualities of Level 4. The mark scheme on page 78 will help you.

Use Sources 1, 2 and 3 and your own knowledge.

Do you agree with the view that the economic policies of the Labour Governments of 1964–1970 were a failure?

The economic policies of the Labour Governments of 1964–1970 were a failure in many ways. Source 2 argues that the Labour Governments 'deteriorated the economical position of Britain'. Evidence of this can be found in the devaluation of the pound and the reduction in the growth of GDP. Additionally, Source 1 draws attention to the failure of the National Plan, describing its success as 'only a moment' and stating that it 'died (possibly murdered) July 1966'. The National Plan was designed to help the economy grow, but it failed to do this. In these ways, the economic policies of the Labour Governments of 1964–1970 failed to achieve their aims.

SOURCE 1

(From Roger Opie, Economic Planning and Growth, *published 1983)*

For many people [the creation of the National Plan] was a great moment. But it was to be only a moment. Indeed one could date the life-cycle of the Plan as 'conceived October 1964, born September 1965, died (possibly murdered) July 1966'.

SOURCE 2

(From Oliver Christi, Successes and Failures of Harold Wilson's Premiership, *published 2009)*

The first years of Harold Wilson's premiership showed some promising political developments and economic progress. However, hopes for a change in the nation's economical position were soon disappointed as the government appeared unable to expand its early success and rather deteriorated the economical position of Britain.

SOURCE 3

(From a speech by Harold Wilson at the Labour Party Conference in 1969)

There is reason for pride in the fact that in the first eight months of this year, our exports are up by 9 per cent over the first eight months of last year. And 30 per cent above the exports for the same months of 1964. And the orders for next year's shipments are rising sharply.

[I draw your attention to] that remarkable statement in *The Economist* newspaper only a few days ago. They confessed that a few weeks earlier they had been expressing deep fears about Britain's economic situation. Now they say, and I quote their words: 'In these past few summer months of 1969, Britain has been running one of the strongest balances of payments among the major powers of the world.'

 Spot the inference

High level answers avoid summarising or paraphrasing the sources, and instead make inferences from the sources. Below is a series of statements. Read Source 3 above and decide which of the statements:

- make inferences from the source (I)
- paraphrase the source (P)
- summarise the source (S)
- cannot be justified from the source (X).

Statement	I	P	S	X
British exports have increased, and Britain's balance of payments situation has improved.				
The increase in exports has improved Britain's balance of payments situation.				
We should feel proud that exports have increased by 9 per cent.				
The Labour Party lost the general election in 1970.				
The improvement in Britain's economic situation was a recent development.				

Labour Government, 1964–1970: Social policy

Social liberalisation

There was considerable liberalisation under Labour in the late 1960s.

■ The Murder Act (1965) suspended all future death sentences. In 1969, the death penalty was abolished.

■ The Race Relations Act (1965) made it illegal to discriminate against people on the grounds of race. It affected public places such as pubs and hotels but did not outlaw racism in housing or employment.

■ The Sexual Offenses Act (1967) legalised private homosexual acts between consenting adult men.

■ The Abortion Act (1967) legalised abortion in some circumstances. It was originally a **Private Member's Bill** but enjoyed considerable support from Labour MPs.

■ The Family Planning Act (1967) committed the NHS to providing contraception.

Welfare

Education

Wilson was prepared to embrace radical educational reform. Labour expanded higher education in the following ways.

■ From 1965, it established new universities, including Kent University.

■ In 1967, the Government announced plans to open 30 **polytechnic colleges**.

■ In 1969, it established the **Open University** to help mature students access higher education.

Secondary education also changed significantly. Anthony Crosland, Labour's Education Minister, argued that the **tripartite** system had created a form of class segregation, as middle-class students tended to attend grammar schools and working-class students secondary moderns. The Government planned to replace the tripartite system with comprehensive schools designed to educate all students in an area, and therefore end the class bias in the education system. The comprehensive scheme was introduced in 1965 but not fully implemented by 1970.

Health and housing

Labour abolished all NHS charges in 1965. However, due to economic problems, Labour was forced to introduce new charges in 1969, which were higher than they had been under the Conservatives.

In 1964, Labour committed to building 500,000 houses a year but, even in 1968 – the high point of Labour's 'housing drive' – financial constraints meant that the Government only built 413,000 houses. Additionally, after the 1968 Ronan Point disaster, where the partial collapse of a 22-storey tower block in East London resulted in the deaths of four people, many criticised the Government for building cheap high density tower blocks.

Unions

Union strike action was seen as an increasing problem during the 1960s. Between 1963 and 1964, around 4 million working days were lost due to strike action; this rose to 11.5 million between 1968 and 1969. Wilson recognised that growing strike action was damaging Britain's economic performance. Barbara Castle, Secretary of State for Employment, proposed a new policy entitled *In Place of Strife* in 1969 which:

■ was designed to limit the power of unions to call strikes

■ proposed that unions should have to ballot members before calling strikes

■ established an Industrial Board with the power to enforce pay settlements on employers and unions.

The plan was highly controversial in the Labour Party and rejected by the **Trades Union Congress**. As a result, *In Place of Strife* never became law. Instead the Government reached a compromise with the TUC that unions would no longer engage in unofficial strikes. This made the Government look weak. The Conservatives claimed that the Labour Government was unwilling and unable to control the unions.

The 1970 election

Wilson called an election in July 1970. Opinion polls suggested that Labour would win as Wilson was more popular than Conservative leader Edward Heath, and Britain had achieved a small balance of payments surplus. Consequently, Wilson expected a Labour victory.

Spectrum of significance

Below is a list of policies and policy areas addressed by the Labour Governments of 1964–1970. Use your own knowledge and the information on pages 36 and 38 to reach a judgement about the level of success of each policy area. Write numbers on the spectrum below to indicate their relative success. Having done this, write a brief justification of your placement, explaining why some of these factors are more important than others. The resulting diagram could form the basis of an essay plan.

Do you agree with the view that the Labour Party policies in the period 1964–1970 were successful?

1. Economic planning
2. Corporatism
3. Industrial policy
4. Education
5. Health and housing
6. Relationship with the unions

Success   Failure

 Write the question   (a)

The following sources relate to the level of success of the Labour Governments of 1964–1970. Read the guidance detailing what you need to know about this topic. Having done this, write an exam-style part (b) question using the sources.

Use Sources 1, 2 and 3 and your own knowledge. Do you agree with the view that …

_____

_____

Explain your answer using Sources 1, 2 and 3 and your own knowledge.

SOURCE 1

(From Peter Dorey, The Labour Governments 1964–1970, *published 2004)*

It is only really in the social sphere that the 1964–1970 Labour Governments can be judged to have achieved notable success, for it is here that several liberal reforms were implemented. Hence it is these social reforms which had partly salvaged the reputation of the 1964–1970 Labour Governments.

SOURCE 2

(From David Marquand, The Progressive Dilemma, *published 1999. Marquand was a Labour MP during this period)*

Few modern British governments have disappointed their supporters more thoroughly than [Harold Wilson's]. The Wilson era was an era of lost innocence, of hopes betrayed.

SOURCE 3

(From Michael Parsons, Harold Wilson and the Labour Government, *published 1999)*

One of the most striking aspects of perceptions of the Wilson Government of 1964–1970 is the contrast between the enthusiasm with which it seemed to begin, and the sense of disappointment or disillusion with which it seemed to end. While Wilson may not have been a great Prime Minister, the achievements were nonetheless significant and may even outweigh the less successful features of the government.

Conservative Government, 1970–1974: Economic policy

The 1970 general election led to a surprise Conservative victory. Edward Heath became Prime Minister with a parliamentary majority of 43.

Break with consensus: 'Selsdon Man'

The Conservative's 1970 **'Selsdon Man'** manifesto was a radical break with the consensus. Essentially, it promised to reduce government intervention in the economy.

The 'Quiet Revolution'

Heath quickly started what he called the 'Quiet Revolution', introducing free market policies by abolishing:

- the NBPI (see page 36), ending government control of the level of prices and incomes
- the IRC (see page 36), ending government subsidies to **'lame duck'** industries.

Anthony Barber's first budget reflected the 'Quiet Revolution' and reduced state intervention by:

- cutting corporation tax and income tax
- ending the provision of free milk to schoolchildren
- cutting government subsidies for council housing rents
- raising prescription charges.

Overall, in 1970, Barber cut government spending by £330 million.

U-turn

Heath's 'Quiet Revolution' did not stimulate economic growth. Instead, unemployment increased, reaching 750,000 in mid-1971 and 1 million by January 1972, along with **inflation**, which reached 15 per cent by the end of 1971. Consequently, government policy changed course during the summer of 1971. By 1972, Heath's critics were accusing him of making a U-turn.

Increased government intervention

Heath tried to end unemployment by returning to high levels of government intervention.

- In 1971, Heath announced a £100 million public works scheme to create jobs in 'Special Development Areas' such as Glasgow, Tyneside and Wearside.
- The Government nationalised struggling industries, including Rolls-Royce in 1971 and the Upper Clyde Shipbuilders in 1972 (see page 36).
- Anthony Barber's 1972 budget cut taxes by £1380 million and increased spending on pensions, the NHS and education. Government spending led to the short-lived 'Barber boom'.

Return to corporatism

Government intervention further increased inflation, which reached twenty per cent in 1972. In response, Heath began working with union and business leaders to agree a voluntary prices and incomes policy. The TUC rejected the policy and refused to do a deal with the Government unless they repealed the Industrial Relations Act (see page 42).

After the failure of the voluntary policy Heath introduced a statutory, three-stage Prices and Incomes Policy.

Stage	Date Introduced	Measures
1	November 1972	All prices, excluding those of fresh vegetables, and all pay was frozen for 90 days.
2	April 1973	The Counter Inflation Act established a Prices Commission and a Pay Board. Wage rises were capped at £250 a year.
3	October 1973	Wage rises were capped at £350 a year.

The three-day week

The 1973 OPEC crisis quadrupled the price of oil. Strike action, which limited the availability of coal, created an energy crisis. The Government responded by declaring a **state of emergency**. Emergency energy-saving measures included:

- reducing the working week to three days
- lowering the speed limit to 50 m.p.h.
- ending television broadcasts at 10.30p.m.

Heath's economic record

Heath's economic policy was largely unsuccessful:

Evidence of success	Evidence of failure
• In 1973, unemployment fell by 20,000.	• Unemployment rose between 1970 and 1973. • Inflation rose throughout. • The Barber boom and the OPEC crisis created a balance of payments crisis in 1973. • Heath abandoned many of his initial policies because they led to rising unemployment and inflation. • The Government was forced to adopt emergency measures during the energy crisis of 1973–1974.

Support or challenge

Below is a sample exam-style part (b) question which asks you how far the sources agree with a specific statement. Below this are three sources which give information relevant to the question. Identify whether the sources support, mainly support, mainly challenge, or challenge the statement in the question and then give reasons for your answer.

Use Sources 1, 2 and 3 and your own knowledge. Do you agree with the view that Edward Heath performed an economic U-turn in the period 1971–1974?

SOURCE 1

(From the Conservative Party election manifesto, 1970)

- We utterly reject the philosophy of wage control.
- We want an economy based on more jobs, higher wages that are well earned, and lower costs.
- We will create the basis for these reductions by cutting out unnecessary state spending.
- We will stop further nationalisation, and create a climate for free enterprise to expand.
- We will reduce taxation.

This source <u>supports / mainly supports / mainly challenges / challenges</u> the view that Edward Heath performed a U-turn in the period 1971–1974 because

_____

_____

SOURCE 2

(From Michael Lynch, Britain 1945–2007, *published 2008)*

Within 18 months of attempting his new style of government, Heath had to turn 180 degrees. Inflation, which had risen to 15 per cent by the end of 1971, and declining industrial output destroyed the government's confidence that they could continue with their original policy. In 1972, the government announced that in an attempt to counter inflation it was returning to a policy of controlling prices and incomes.

This source <u>supports / mainly supports / mainly challenges / challenges</u> the view that Edward Heath performed a U-turn in the period 1971–1974 because

_____

_____

SOURCE 3

(From a lecture on Edward Heath given by Professor John Ramsden, 2006)

Heath was not an idealist. He would ditch any policy that was not achieving the result aimed for. Heath's objective was always economic growth, low prices and reduced unemployment, and any tools would do if they might build such a package.

This source <u>supports / mainly supports / mainly challenges / challenges</u> the view that Edward Heath performed a U-turn in the period 1971–1974 because

_____

_____

 Add own knowledge

On this page are a sample exam-style part (b) question and the three sources referred to in the question. In one colour, draw links between the sources to show ways in which they agree about the extent to which Edward Heath performed an economic U-turn in the period 1971–1974. In another colour, draw links between the sources to show ways in which they disagree. Around the edge of the sources, write relevant own knowledge. Again, draw links to show the ways in which this agrees and disagrees with the sources.

Conservative Government, 1970–1974: Heath and the unions

Revised

Industrial relations

In 1971, Heath initiated trade union reform. The Industrial Relations Act (1971) created the National Industrial Relations Court, which was empowered to:

- halt strike action for 60 days to allow for negotiation
- order ballots to ensure strikes reflected the wishes of union members.

Additionally, strikes were outlawed as part of Heath's Prices and Incomes Policy (see page 40).

Success and failure

Unions opposed the Industrial Relations Act and refused to co-operate with the Government's attempt to create a voluntary incomes policy in 1972.

The Industrial Relations Act also proved to be unenforceable. During Heath's Government there were several major strikes, including two important strikes organised by the National Union of Mineworkers (NUM) (see boxes).

The role of Edward Heath

Though Heath's biggest success was negotiating Britain's entry to the EEC in 1972 (Britain joined on 1 January 1973), Heath is often remembered as one of the least successful Prime Ministers. This is due to his lack of skill in handling the media and his inability to set out his political vision. He also played a role in the failure of his Government.

- He quickly abandoned his original economic policies and therefore gained a reputation for inconsistency and a lack of courage.
- His union policies antagonised the unions, worsening industrial relations.
- As a result of industrial disputes, between February 1972 and February 1974 Heath declared a state of emergency five times. The public came to associate the Government with crisis measures.

Heath's Government was also unfortunate in that it had to deal with the OPEC crisis.

Heath's critics

Wilson and the Labour Party criticised Heath for the following reasons.

- They argued that the Industrial Relations Act attempted to strip trade unions of their traditional rights.
- Trade unions refused to co-operate with Heath's voluntary prices and incomes policy unless the Government repealed the Industrial Relations Act.
- Wilson argued that growing unemployment and Heath's U-turn showed how Conservative economic policy was failing.
- Wilson argued that Heath's policy of big cuts in 1970, followed by big spending increases in 1971–1972, was a return to 'stop-go' economics.

Even Conservatives attacked Heath:

- **One Nation Conservatives** argued that Heath's refusal to help failing industries in the north risked destroying working-class communities.
- Right-wing Conservatives were only prepared to back Heath's prices and incomes policy as a temporary measure. They wanted to go back to free market policies once economic stability was restored.

1972 miners' strike

In January 1972, the NUM rejected the **Coal Board**'s annual pay offer. Consequently, 280,000 miners went on strike for six weeks until the miners accepted a pay rise three times higher than originally offered.

1974 miners' strike

In November 1973, the NUM rejected the Coal Board's pay offer again. The threat of a strike at a time when oil prices were extremely high led Heath to declare a state of emergency to keep key industries running (see page 40). The NUM called a full-scale strike in February 1974. Heath refused the miners' demands and called a general election to generate public support for the Government. However, Heath narrowly lost the election and, to restore coal supplies and settle the dispute, the new Labour Government settled the miners' strike.

Below are a sample exam-style part (a) question and two paragraphs written in answer to this question. Read the question and the two answers, as well as the sources. Then, using a highlighter, highlight examples of integration – where sources are used together. You cannot reach Level 3 or Level 4 of the part (a) mark scheme (see page 78) without integration of the sources. Which paragraph reaches the higher level?

Study Sources 1, 2 and 3.

How far do the sources agree in their assessment of Edward Heath's character?

Sample 1

All three sources agree that there were positive aspects to Edward Heath's character. Sources 1 and 3 agree that, as a politician, he had the best interests of the country at heart. For example, Source 1 describes Heath as 'a man of serious purpose and absolute integrity of character'. Similarly, Source 3 states, 'There is no doubting Ted Heath's sympathy for people'. Together, these sources suggest that he was compassionate and dedicated in his approach to leadership. Additionally, all three sources suggest that Edward Heath could be good company. Source 1 states that on occasion, 'one would think, "Oh, what a nice man Ted is"'. This is supported by the accounts of Source 2 and Source 3. Source 2 remembers Heath greeting people 'with a great chuckle and much heaving of the shoulders', and in Source 3 Jack Jones states that he 'quickly established a feeling of friendship with Heath' and that Heath 'cheerfully' played him Labour's national anthem. In this way, the sources agree that Heath was committed to leading the country well, and that he could be pleasant to be around.

Sample 2

All three sources agree that there were positive aspects to Edward Heath's character. Source 1 describes him as 'a man of serious purpose and absolute integrity of character', suggesting that, as a politician, he had the best interests of the country at heart. In addition, Source 1 states that on occasion, 'one would think, "Oh, what a nice man Ted is"'. Source 2 agrees that he could be nice, explaining that sometimes he would greet people 'with a great chuckle and much heaving of the shoulders'. Finally, Source 3 provides evidence that he was both compassionate and good company. The source states, 'There is no doubting Ted Heath's sympathy for people', and describes him playing the Labour national anthem on his new piano. In this way, all three sources provide evidence that Edward Heath could be pleasant and sympathetic.

SOURCE 1

(From William Rees-Mogg, Memoirs, *published 2001. Rees-Mogg was editor of* The Times *from 1967–1981.)*

As a prime minister [Edward Heath] was a man of serious purpose and absolute integrity of character. However, he lacked flexibility. He was not good with people. Indeed, he was very bad with his enemies. There was variability in his treatment of everyone. On one day, his temperament would be pleasant and warm, and one would think, 'Oh, what a nice man Ted is'; on another day one would meet him, he would be cold and distant.

SOURCE 2

(From John Barnes, Edward Heath: A personal recollection, *published 2005. Barnes worked as an advisor to Edward Heath during his time as Prime Minister)*

You could never be certain just how he was going to greet you. On occasion it was with a great chuckle and much heaving of the shoulders, but at other moments, he was curt, almost as if he had never met you before. Briefing him was surprisingly difficult because he would sit impassively, never offering any comment or interjection or indeed a reaction of any kind.

SOURCE 3

(From Jack Jones, Union Man, *published 1986. Jones was General Secretary of the Transport and General Workers' Union from 1968 until 1978. Here he remembers an evening with Ted Heath in 1969)*

There is no doubting Ted Heath's sympathy for people and we quickly established a feeling of friendship. It was a pleasant evening, with Heath talking of his yacht and musical interests. At one stage he showed us a new piano he had bought and at our invitation played one or two short pieces. Then another member of the group called out, 'Play the "Red Flag" for Jack' and the leader of the Tory Party cheerfully played Labour's national anthem.

Labour Government, 1974–1979: Economic policy

The February 1974 election resulted in a **hung parliament**. Heath failed to form a government and therefore Wilson returned as Prime Minister, leading a **minority government**. Without a parliamentary majority, Wilson was forced to call a new election in October 1974, which resulted in a Labour majority of three seats.

Wilson continued as Prime Minister until March 1976, when he resigned and was replaced by James Callaghan.

Economic policy

The new Government had a series of economic priorities:

- end the miner's strike
- reduce unemployment
- reduce inflation
- reduce the balance of payments deficit.

Union and pay policy

Labour repealed the Industrial Relations Act and proposed greater co-operation between the Government and trade union movement. Labour's initial policy, the Social Contract, was a voluntary incomes policy. The Government asked unions to exercise pay restraint in return for a 'social wage', essentially offering to subsidise the cost of transport and council housing.

By June 1975, **wage inflation** had reached 33 per cent. Recognising that the Social Contract had failed, Wilson now introduced a compulsory incomes policy. In July 1975, the Government enforced a pay freeze for everyone who earned more than £8600 a year. This frustrated the unions. The compulsory incomes policy continued until Labour's defeat in 1979. During this period pay was never allowed to rise more than 10 per cent a year.

Monetarism

Denis Healey, Labour's new Chancellor, broke with the consensus by embracing **monetarism**. In 1975, he argued it was no longer the Government's policy to spend money to promote employment.

Instead, the Government needed to control inflation by cutting government spending. His 1976 budget aimed to cut government spending by £2.5 billion in two years.

IMF crisis

Britain's economic problems led to a fall in the value of the pound. In January 1976, the pound was worth just over $2. However, by September it was worth only $1.63. To defend the value of the pound the Government borrowed £3900 million from the **International Monetary Fund (IMF)**. The Government had to agree to cut £3000 million from public spending to get the loan.

The 'Winter of Discontent'

In August 1978, Callaghan introduced his new incomes policy, restricting pay rises to five per cent a year, which angered the public and the unions. In early 1979, public sector unions **NUPE** and **COHSE** went on strike for six weeks, in a period which became known as the 'Winter of Discontent'. This affected rubbish collection, sewage treatment and burial of the dead. Eventually, a pay deal of 9 per cent was agreed and the strike was called off. Nonetheless, the strike was very unpopular and therefore extremely damaging for Callaghan's Government.

Labour's economic record

Labour had a mixed record between 1974 and 1979.

Evidence of success	Evidence of failure
• Inflation fell from 16% in 1974 to 8% in 1979. • Britain's balance of payments position improved from a £3.6 billion deficit in 1974 to a £0.8 billion surplus in 1978. • Government spending fell from 56% of GDP in 1976 to 51% of GDP in 1979.	• Unemployment rose from 628,000 in 1974 to 1,464,000 in 1979. • The number of days lost through strike action increased from 14,750,000 in 1974 to 29,474,000 in 1979.

Doing reliability well   (a)

Below are a series of definitions listing common reasons why sources are reliable or unreliable, and a series of sources. Under Source 1, explain why the source is either reliable or unreliable for the purpose stated, justifying your answer by referring to the following definitions.

- **Vested interest**: the source is written so that the writer can protect their power or their financial interests.
- **Second-hand report**: the writer of the source is not an eyewitness, but is relying on someone else's account.
- **Expertise**: the source is written on a subject on which the author (for example, a historian) is an expert.
- **Political bias**: a source is written by a politician and it reflects their political views.
- **Reputation**: a source is written to protect the writer's reputation.

SOURCE 1

(From the Conservative Party election manifesto, 1979)

The Labour Party has made things worse in three ways. First, by actively discouraging the creation of wealth.

Second, by enlarging the role of the State.

Third, by heaping privilege without responsibility on the trade unions, Labour have given a minority of extremists the power to abuse individual liberties and to thwart Britain's chances of success.

It is not just that Labour have governed Britain badly. They have reached a dead-end.

> The source is reliable / fairly reliable / fairly unreliable / unreliable as evidence of the impact of the economic policies of the Labour Governments in the period 1974–1979 because
>
> _____
>
> _____

SOURCE 2

(From Richard Seymour, The Meaning of David Cameron, *published 2010)*

The 1974–1979 Labour government failed to deliver on its radical agenda. Its spending cuts, its imposition of wage cuts, and its prolonged, bitter wars with organised labour, simply demoralised the working class.

SOURCE 3

(From Tom Pettinger, Jim Callaghan: A Successful Prime Minister, *published 2010)*

Callaghan held successes throughout his term in office – inflation fell from 16% and 24% the two previous years before he took office, down to nearly 8% in 1979. The Callaghan government can be said to have left the economy in a better condition in 1979 than they had found it in 1974. However, whilst Callaghan was successful to an extent, there were clear failings; his premiership is tainted by the IMF crisis which is seen to be a blot on his economic record. Also Callaghan's handling of the disastrous Winter of Discontent is seen to be poor.

Develop the detail   (a)

Below are a sample exam-style part (b) question and a paragraph written in answer to this question. The question refers to the sources on this page. The paragraph contains a limited amount of own knowledge. Annotate the paragraph to add additional own knowledge to the answer.

Use Sources 1, 2 and 3 and your own knowledge.

Do you agree with the view that the economic policies of the Labour Governments in the period 1974–1979 were unsuccessful?

> One way in which the Labour Government's economic policies were unsuccessful was the handling of relations with the trade unions. Source 2 argues that evidence of failure can be found in the 'prolonged, bitter wars with organised labour'. These disputes continued until the Winter of Discontent in 1979. Source 3 describes Callaghan's handling of this period as 'poor'. The Winter of Discontent followed Callaghan's decision to restrict pay rises to five per cent a year. Source 3 refers to the impact of these strikes, accusing the trade unions of '[thwarting] Britain's chances of success'. In this way, the economic policies of the Labour Governments of 1974–1979 were unsuccessful in the sense that they led to prolonged disputes with the unions, which hindered Britain's economic growth.

Social policy, 1970–1979

Heath's social policy, 1970–1974

Education

Margaret Thatcher, Heath's Minister for Education and Science, made a number of significant changes in the British Education system.

- She continued the transition from selective education to a comprehensive system and was broadly successful in doing so. Under the Conservatives, the proportion of 11 to 16-year-olds in comprehensive education shot up from almost one-third to over two-thirds. Notably, Conservative areas, such as Bexley in Kent, refused to abandon the selective system.
- In 1971, she introduced the 1971 Milk Act, which ended the provision of free school milk. In addition, she raised the price of school meals.
- In 1973, she raised the school leaving age from 15 to 16.

Thatcher also announced a 40 per cent increase in the budget for building new polytechnic colleges.

Health care

Sir Keith Joseph, Minister for Health, introduced a major NHS reform in 1973. The National Health Service Reorganisation Act was designed to save the Government money by restructuring the NHS. The Act set up new Area Health Authorities designed to manage the provision of health care in each county.

In the short term, spending on the NHS increased. Critics argued that the policy led to a '**bureaucratisation**' of the NHS. Indeed, the proportion of NHS money spent on administration grew in relation to the proportion spent on patient care.

Labour social policy, 1974–1979

Education

Labour's February 1974 manifesto committed the party to ending selection and expanding nursery education. However, Wilson made it clear that there would be no legislation to force local authorities to introduce comprehensive education.

Callaghan took a more active approach to the Government's education policy. His 1976 Education Act targeted local authorities that still operated the selective system. The Act was designed to force them to publish a timetable for introducing comprehensive education.

Callaghan also addressed education in his 1976 'Ruskin Speech'. In essence, the speech attacked underperforming teachers and called for higher standards in schools. The speech reflected a growing public anxiety about falling standards and 'trendy', but ineffective, teaching methods.

Health care

The February 1974 Labour manifesto promised huge increases in spending on the NHS. Wilson ensured that this promise was kept. Indeed, the years 1974 to 1976 saw average spending increases of 5 per cent, the largest ever increases in NHS spending.

The Labour Government implemented Joseph's National Health Service Reorganisation Act. Consequently, there was a 300 per cent increase in NHS administrative staff between 1968 and 1979.

Finally, the Junior Minister for Health, Dr David Owen, established the Resources Allocation Working Party (RAWP). The RAWP devised a new formula for distributing resources within the NHS, which meant that more money went to working-class areas.

Support or challenge?

Below is a sample exam-style part (a) question which asks you how far the sources agree with a specific statement. Below this are three sources which give information relevant to the question. Identify whether the sources support, mainly support, mainly challenge, or challenge the statement in the question and then give reasons for your answer.

Study Sources 1, 2 and 3.

How far do the sources suggest that the benefits of the 1971 Milk Act outweighed the costs?

SOURCE 1

(From the recollections of a Scottish housewife)

If I were to sum up one memory of Thatcher, it's that she took away our milk. Our free milk at school that we so desperately needed. As impoverished kids coming from a very working class background (so working class that nobody actually had a job) our milk each day was essential for nutrition. For many, it really was the only meal of the day.

> This source supports / mainly supports / mainly challenges / challenges the view that the benefits of the 1971 Milk Act outweighed the costs because
>
> _____
>
> _____

SOURCE 2

(From The Times*, 18 December 1971)*

Figures released this week by the Milk Marketing Board for November show that the supply of free school milk has dropped by more than two million gallons compared with the same month last year. However, total milk sales dropped by only 1.6 million gallons, indicating that domestic sales have increased.

Mr Ivan Fagent, head of the Milk Marketing Board's education and nutrition department, said: 'The figures are considerably better than we expected and must reflect the fact that a lot of people who were getting free milk are prepared to pay for it.'

> This source supports / mainly supports / mainly challenges / challenges the view that the benefits of the 1971 Milk Act outweighed the costs because
>
> _____
>
> _____

SOURCE 3

(From a BBC news broadcast, 15 June 1971)

Mrs Thatcher has argued that ending free milk for all but nursery and primary children will free more money to spend on other areas of education, like new buildings. In a full year the saving on milk provision will be about £9m.

> This source supports / mainly supports / mainly challenges / challenges the view that the benefits of the 1971 Milk Act outweighed the costs because
>
> _____
>
> _____

 Linking sources

Above are a sample exam-style part (a) question and the three sources referred to in the question. In one colour, draw links between the sources to show ways in which they agree about the benefits of the 1971 Milk Act outweighing the costs. In another colour, draw links between the sources to show ways in which they disagree.

Labour Government, 1974–1979: Wilson and Callaghan

Revised

The role of Harold Wilson

'MacWilson'

Wilson, much like Macmillan (see page 28), was committed to maintaining consensus policies and continued many of Macmillan's policies. Some commentators even described the new Prime Minister as 'MacWilson'.

Media management

Between 1963 and 1966, Wilson excelled at using the media. He believed that the press were biased towards the Conservatives, but he could influence television news to favour Labour. He successfully worked with media professionals to perfect his television manner. However, during 1966 he became convinced that television executives were against him, and made less use of it.

'Kitchen Cabinet'

Wilson had few allies at the top of the Labour Party. Therefore, he tended to seek advice from a group of friends and advisors who became known as the 'Kitchen Cabinet'. Wilson's reliance on his 'Kitchen Cabinet', particularly his Personal Secretary Marcia Williams, led to accusations of **cronyism**.

'The pound in your pocket'

Wilson's reputation was damaged by his handling of the 1967 devaluation. In a television broadcast he assured the public that 'the pound in your pocket has not been devalued', but as imports became more expensive it was clear that this was false. The broadcast led the public to lose trust in Wilson.

Labour factions

One of Wilson's greatest gifts was uniting the different factions of the Labour Party. Wilson was generally able to work out compromises, or find ways of presenting policies, which kept the Left and Right wings of the party together. For example, when the Labour Party was split over the issue of staying in the EEC in 1975, Wilson called a referendum. This delivered a clear result in favour of membership and settled the issue.

The role of James Callaghan

Personal appeal

Callaghan's down-to-earth style made him very popular with British voters. They also recognised his experience as, before becoming Prime Minister, he had been Chancellor, Foreign Secretary and Home Secretary. Finally, Callaghan was popular because he was known as a moderate. Indeed, he defeated the left-wing candidates Tony Benn and Michael Foot in the 1976 Labour leadership election.

Union man

Callaghan was widely regarded as a loyal supporter of the unions. For example, in 1969 he led the Cabinet opposition to Wilson's attempts at union reform (see page 44). He therefore enjoyed the trust of most union leaders, which helped him in negotiations with them.

Pragmatist

Callaghan was also a pragmatist. When it became clear that the Government could no longer spend its way out of economic trouble he willingly abandoned **Keynesianism** in favour of monetarism.

Problems in Parliament

During the 1970s, Wilson and Callaghan both had difficulty managing Parliament. Labour's slight majority soon disappeared due to the deaths of Labour MPs and **by-election** defeats. By 1977, Callaghan headed a minority government. From March 1977 to September 1978, the Government had a majority of support in Parliament due to the **Lib–Lab Pact**. However, even with Liberal support, it was difficult for the Government to get controversial laws passed by Parliament. Consequently, Callaghan suffered a record 34 defeats in Parliament, in contrast to Eden, Macmillan and Home, who were never defeated in Parliament.

RAG – Rate the timeline

Below are a sample exam question and a timeline. Read the question, study the timeline and, using three coloured pens, put a red, amber or green star next to the events to show:

- **Red:** Events and policies that have no relevance to the question
- **Amber:** Events and policies that have some significance to the question
- **Green:** Events and policies that are directly relevant to the question

1) Do you agree with the view that the economic policies of the Labour governments in the period 1964–1979 were a success?

Now repeat the activity with the following questions:

2) Do you agree with the view that failures of economic policy were the main reason why the period 1964–1979 witnessed considerable political uncertainty?

3) Do you agree with the view that the relationship between the Government and the trade unions deteriorated in the period 1964–1979?

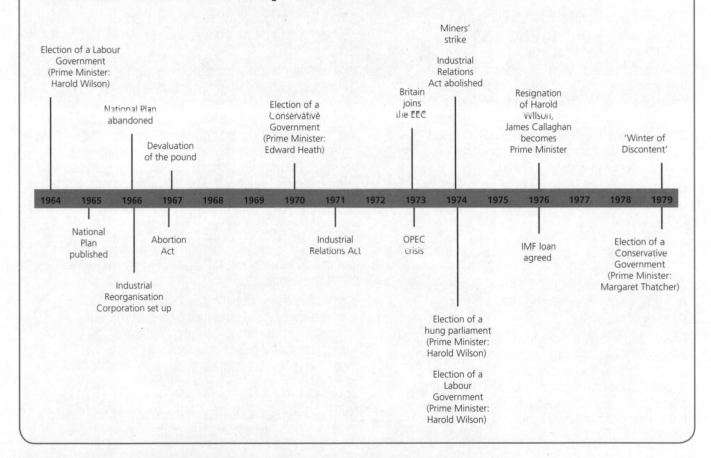

Recommended reading

Below is a list of suggested further reading on this topic.

- *Britain 1945–2007*, pages 80–109, Michael Lynch (2008)
- *Hope and Glory: Britain 1900–2000*, Chapters 9 and 10, Peter Clark (2004)
- *A History of 20th Century Britain*, Part 3, Andrew Marr (2011)

Section 3: Exam focus

Revised

On pages 51–53 are sample answers to the exam-style questions on this page.
Read the answers and the examiner comments around them.

a) Study Sources 1, 2 and 3.

How far do the sources suggest that the 1970 Conservative election victory was
a 'personal victory' for Edward Heath? Explain your answer using the evidence
of Sources 1, 2 and 3. **(20 marks)**

b) Use Sources 4, 5 and 6 and your own knowledge.

Do you agree with the view that Harold Wilson was an ineffective Prime Minister
in the years 1964–1970? Explain your answer using Sources 4, 5 and 6 and your
own knowledge. **(40 marks)**

SOURCE 1

(From a BBC election report published in 1997)

The election result was a deep shock for Labour,
and for the pollsters. The low turnout certainly
didn't help Labour and the poor trade figures
released just three days before polling may
have been the deciding factor for many floating
voters when choosing between Labour and
Conservative. The figures backed up Conservative
claims that the economy would suffer if Labour
should win again.

For Edward Heath, derided by many
commentators, the election represented a
personal victory.

SOURCE 2

*(Sara Morrison, Vice-Chair of the Conservative
Party 1970–1975 recalls the 1970 election
campaign in 2013)*

I was set upon by people from all over the country
who said 'Heath was the drawback', because
of his lack of vision and his inability to express
himself. Conservative candidates were tearing
his picture out of the manifesto before putting
it through people's doors because Ted was a
complete turn off.

SOURCE 3

*(From The Times, 20 June 1970, the day following
the 1970 general election)*

At 1.16 a.m. it was all over. The national swing to
the Conservatives was so decisive that Mr Heath
changed his plans and headed for London.

The campaign that failed for Labour has been
pinned firmly to Mr Wilson. He felt certain of
success if the electorate were given the choice:
Wilson or Heath. The bad trade figures, only three
days before polling, caused apprehension at
Labour Head Office. It was all Mr Heath needed to
illustrate their warnings about the economy.

SOURCE 4

(From John Major, Tony Blair and the Conflict of
Leadership: Collision Course, *Michael Foley, published
2002)*

The Wilson government suffered a number of policy
setbacks, such as industrial relations problems, the
devaluation of the pound, and the failure of economic
planning. As Prime Minister, he became an isolated
figure. The high hopes and idealistic expectations of 1964
were gradually eroded by the actions of a government
facing immense difficulties. Harold Wilson gained a
reputation for pragmatism and flexibility that too often
looked like evasion, delay and short-term compromise.

SOURCE 5

(From Peter Dorey (ed.), The Labour Governments: 1964–
1970, *published 2006)*

Some historians are willing to look past Wilson's
bad reputation, and emphasise his government's
successes, often achieved in spite of extremely difficult
circumstances. Against the common charge that Wilson
was unprincipled some historians suggest that on a
number of occasions Wilson suffered by being too
principled for his own good. Indeed, they point to his
stubborn refusal to devalue the pound and his dogged
pursuit of industrial relations reform in 1969.

SOURCE 6

*(From Harold Wilson's television address following the
devaluation of the pound, 19 November 1967)*

By our policies and by the efforts of our people, we have
reduced the trade deficit, the deficit we inherited three
years ago. Our exports have risen by double the rate
of the last few years. No one could doubt, at home or
abroad, our determination to win through.

Our decision to devalue attacks our problems at the root.
From now on the pound abroad is worth 14 per cent
less. That doesn't mean that the pound in your pocket or
purse has been devalued. What it does mean is that we
shall be able to sell more abroad on a competitive basis.

a) Study Sources 1, 2 and 3.

How far do the sources suggest that the 1970 Conservative election victory was a 'personal victory' for Edward Heath? Explain your answer using the evidence of Sources 1, 2 and 3. (**20 marks**)

All three sources suggest that Heath played a significant role in the 1970 general election campaign. However, only Sources 1 and 3 strongly support the idea that the Conservative's election win was a 'personal victory' for Edward Heath.

Source 1 clearly states that 'For Edward Heath ... the election represented a personal victory'. This is supported by Source 3 which indicates that Heath played a major role in the last stages of the campaign using the trade figures to illustrate his 'warnings about the economy'. Source 1 also shows that the election campaign was extremely personal. It argues that this was central to Wilson's election campaign as he 'felt certain of success if the electorate were given the choice: Wilson or Heath'. Source 2 indicates that Heath's personality was also important to the Conservative campaign as his photograph was on the front cover of the manifesto. Therefore, Sources 1, 2 and 3 also acknowledge that the 1970 election was, in part, about a choice between Heath and Wilson and therefore that Heath's victory was a personal triumph.

Nonetheless, there is evidence that the Conservative victory was not a true triumph for Heath. Source 2 indicates that Heath was seen as a liability even by his own party. Source 2, written by a senior Conservative, is clear, 'people from all over the country who said "Heath was the drawback"'. However, Source 2 is the account of Sara Morrison, the Vice-Chair of the Conservative Party from 1970–1975. During this period Heath performed a U-turn and many of his policies failed. Therefore, this may have influenced her view of his performance in the 1970 election. Consequently, the rejection of Heath in 1970 that she describes may not be wholly accurate. Nonetheless, Source 3 indicates that this was the view of the Labour leadership too as Labour's campaign had 'been pinned firmly to Mr Wilson'. Additionally, Sources 1 and 3 indicate that Heath won due to Labour's failings rather than his own appeal. Both sources argue that bad economic news led many to turn away from Labour. Specifically, Source 3 points to 'bad trade figures' and also considers the timing of the news, which was released 'only three days before polling', noting that this gave Heath an important weapon in the last stage of the campaign.

Overall, all three sources indicate that Heath played an important role in the campaign. Finally, although Sources 1 and 3 point to the importance of other factors such as the later trade figures, it is clear that Heath played a big role in the victory as he skilfully used the bad economic news to underline his ongoing message: the failings of Labour. In this sense and in light of the highly personal nature of the 1970 campaign mentioned by all three sources, the 1970 election campaign was clearly a 'personal victory' for Edward Heath.

The introduction provides a brief answer to the question by summarising the overall position of each source.

This paragraph begins with the best evidence from the sources that supports the statement in the question.

The candidate immediately supports the argument of Source 1 with evidence from Source 3, showing detailed cross referencing from the start.

The essay questions the reliability of Source 2 by referring to its provenance, and by comparing it to Sources 1 and 3.

The conclusion is consistent with the introduction and evaluates 'how far' the election was a personal victory for Heath by showing how he used the trade figures to his advantage in the final stages of the campaign.

17/20

This essay gets a mark in Level 4 because it contains a detailed comparison of the sources, with a strong focus on the question. It considers provenance to weigh the reliability of the sources and ends with a conclusion that addresses 'how far' the sources agree that the 1970 victory was a personal victory for Edward Heath.

b) Use Sources 4, 5 and 6 and your own knowledge.

Do you agree with the view that Harold Wilson was an ineffective Prime Minister in the years 1964–1970? Explain your answer using Sources 4, 5 and 6 and your own knowledge. **(40 marks)**

Harold Wilson was a broadly ineffective Prime Minister in the years 1964–1970. As Source 4 argues, many of his policies were unsuccessful, and he had a reputation for compromise and evasion. However, Source 5 is correct to argue that Wilson was dealing with difficult circumstances and therefore that his failures reflect the problems that he was dealing with rather than his own effectiveness as a Prime Minister. Nonetheless, there is clearly some truth in the idea that Wilson was an ineffective Prime Minister as he was unable to deliver on several of his key goals, such as maintaining the value of the pound, which is mentioned in Source 6.

Source 4 argues that Wilson experienced many economic difficulties, including 'industrial relations problems, the devaluation of the pound, and the failure of economic planning'. Source 4 is correct to argue that economic planning was a failure. Wilson was elected in 1964 promising to increase the emphasis on economic planning. Indeed, in 1964 he introduced the Department for Economic Affairs (DEA) which was given the task of devising and implementing a National Economic Plan. However, the plan was a failure, because after its publication in September 1965 it was abandoned in July 1966 due to the fact that it was based on overly optimistic assumptions about the performance of the economy. In this sense Wilson was an ineffective Prime Minister because he failed to deliver on the 'high hopes and idealistic expectations of 1964' (Source 4) for a more efficient and better planned Britain.

Beyond planning, Wilson's economic policy had other problems. Source 6 is taken from a speech Wilson made following the 1967 devaluation of the pound. As Source 5 argues, Wilson had been committed to keeping the pound at its previous value. However, in 1967 he was forced to drop the value of the pound from $2.80 to $2.40. Other economic problems included the slow growth of British GDP. Wilson had pledged to achieve a growth rate of over 4 per cent. However, in 1969 growth was a mere 1.9 per cent.

Even so, as Source 5 argues, Wilson was battling with 'extremely difficult circumstances'. The British economy had been declining relative to other economies since the early 1950s. For example, while Britain was only growing at a rate of three per cent, France was growing at 5 per cent, West Germany was growing at 6 per cent and Japan was growing at 9.4 per cent. Additionally, Britain's growth rate slowed in the later 1950s and by 1963 unemployment was at a post-war high of 878,000, and economic growth had slowed to 2 per cent. Therefore, Source 5 argues that Wilson's successes were even more remarkable. Wilson's economic policy did have some successes. For example, in 1968 the British economy grew by 4.1 per cent, and in 1969, Britain achieved a balance of payments surplus of £445 million. Therefore, as Source 5 argues, Wilson's successes indicate that he

The introduction uses all three sources and recognises that there could be a difference between Wilson's reputation and his actual achievements. Even so, it reaches a clear conclusion that Wilson did fail in key areas.

This paragraph is structured so that it begins with the argument of a source and then continues to support the argument with accurate and relevant detail.

This paragraph extends the previous one by considering other aspects of Wilson's economic policy.

Here, the candidate weighs the argument presented in Source 5 by considering detailed information from own knowledge.

was an effective Prime Minister, because he did boost economic growth and exports in very difficult circumstances.

However, Wilson was not viewed as successful because he lost the trust of the British people. Source 4 argues that he gained a reputation for 'evasion, delay and short-term compromise'. Source 6, Wilson's speech about devaluation, supports this. Wilson famously claimed that devaluation did not 'mean that the pound in your pocket or purse has been devalued'. However, as imports became more expensive following devaluation, many felt that Wilson had not told the whole truth. Wilson's reputation was also damaged because of his 'Kitchen Cabinet', a group of friends and advisors who Wilson relied on more than his Cabinet colleagues, including his Personal Secretary Marcia Williams. Wilson's relationship with Williams led to accusations of cronyism. Clearly, as Source 4 argues, Wilson was not an effective Prime Minister because trust in his government was 'gradually eroded' (Source 4).

Nonetheless, Source 5 argues that Wilson's 'unprincipled' reputation may well reflect his ability to compromise. Source 5 argues that Wilson was a man of principle, who was committed to important policies. Indeed, two of his most significant policy failures reflected his 'stubborn refusal' to give up on his principles. First, Source 5 refers to 'industrial relations reform'. Wilson's reforms were known as In Place of Strife. However, Wilson was unable to persuade his own party or the unions to accept the reform and therefore the proposals had to be dropped. Equally, Wilson was committed to the principle of maintaining the value of the pound. In both cases, Wilson's inability to achieve success indicates that he was an ineffective Prime Minister because he was not able to achieve his own most important goals.

In conclusion, Wilson did have some successes and these indicate that he was not wholly ineffective as a Prime Minister. Economic figures from 1968 and 1969 show that under Wilson the economy did grow more quickly than before while at the same time a balance of payments surplus was generated. However, Wilson's reputation for cronyism and evasion and his inability to achieve key policy goals such as economic planning, industrial relations reform and maintaining the value of the pound explain why he has a reputation as an ineffective leader.

Here the candidate returns to the idea that Wilson failed to achieve some of his most important policy aims. The two examples used come from Source 5, but the candidate builds on these with detailed own knowledge.

The conclusion is balanced as it recognises Wilson's successes and failures. However, it concludes with a clear judgement that his inability to achieve his key goals explains his reputation as an ineffective leader.

37/40

This essay is strong in terms of own knowledge and the use of the sources. Own knowledge is detailed, precise, accurate and focused. Additionally, the essay is extremely well structured. The candidate has selected information from the sources to support and challenge the view expressed in the question, and gains a mark in Level 4 by weighing the evidence of the sources in paragraph 3 and in the conclusion. However, the essay does not get full marks as the sources are not fully integrated into the essay.

Reverse engineering

The best essays are based on careful plans. Read the essay and the examiner's comments and try to work out the general points of the plan used to write the essay. Once you have done this, note down the specific examples used to support each general point.

Section 4: End of consensus: Thatcher in power, 1979–1990

The general election of 1979 resulted in a Conservative victory and Margaret Thatcher subsequently won two further elections. The Conservatives gained an overall majority in Parliament every time.

General election	Conservative majority
1979	44 seats
1983	144 seats
1987	102 seats

Thatcher's three terms

Thatcher's focus changed over time.

- In her first term the Government's top priority was controlling **inflation** using monetarist policies.

- In her second term the Government attempted to revitalise the British economy through a range of free market policies, including **privatisation** and union reform.

- Her final term saw reforms in education, health care and local government.

Causes of the 1979 victory

The Conservative victory was largely due to the perceived failures of the Labour Government (see pages 44–48). Labour was blamed for:

- the Winter of Discontent
- the IMF crisis
- rising unemployment
- the strict incomes policy
- rising union militancy
- rising inflation.

Additionally, the Conservative's 'Labour isn't working' campaign successfully emphasised Labour's failure to restore full employment.

The origins of Thatcherism

Thatcher and her chief Conservative allies were influenced by **New Right** thinkers. For example, she agreed with Friedrich Hayek that state economic control was the enemy of individual freedom. Hayek pointed to Nazi Germany and Stalin's Russia as two historical examples of countries where state control of the economy had led to the destruction of individual rights. Thatcher, like Hayek, argued that a free economy was the foundation of individual freedom.

Thatcherism and consensus politics

Thatcher deliberately set out to break with consensus politics. She rejected key aspects of the **post-war settlement**, including the view that the Government was responsible for creating full employment. She also rejected **Keynesianism** and **corporatism**, the methods that post-war Governments had used to try to ensure full employment was achieved.

Thatcher believed that consensus was a sign of weakness. She meant this in two ways.

- First, she believed consensus essentially meant compromise. She viewed compromise as weakness, because she believed strong leaders passionately followed their convictions. Indeed, she described herself as a 'conviction politician'.

- Second, she believed that consensus policies had weakened Britain. She argued that until 1945 Britain had been a leading world power, but consensus policies from 1945 to 1979 failed to maintain Britain's status. In fact, Thatcher argued that the post-war consensus had been an attempt to 'manage decline' rather than defend or enhance Britain's world role.

Finally, Thatcher believed that the post-war consensus was wrong because consensus politics was essentially a form of socialism. Thatcher equated socialism with state control of the economy, and therefore rejected **nationalisation** and corporatism, policies which increased the Government's economic control.

Thatcher and post-war history

Thatcher was highly critical of Britain's post-war political leaders, including many Conservative Prime Ministers. For Thatcher, the Suez Crisis of 1957 (see page 28), Heath's 1972 U-turn (see page 40), and Health's inability to defeat the NUM in 1974 (see page 42) were clear examples of failure. She was determined not to repeat the mistakes of the past.

Mind map

Use the information on the opposite page and in the previous section of this book to add detail to the mind map below.

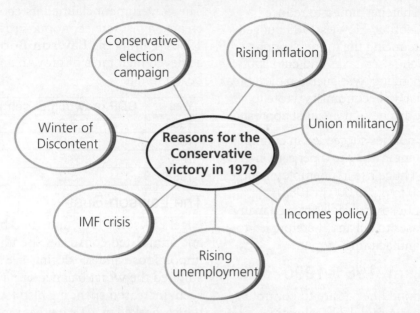

Conservative election campaign

Rising inflation

Winter of Discontent

Reasons for the Conservative victory in 1979

Union militancy

IMF crisis

Incomes policy

Rising unemployment

Add own knowledge

Below are a sample exam-style part (b) question and the three sources referred to in the question. In one colour, draw links between the sources to show ways in which they agree about the reasons for the Conservative victory in 1979. In another colour, draw links between the sources to show ways in which they disagree. Around the edge of the sources, write relevant own knowledge. Again, draw links to show the ways in which this agrees and disagrees with the sources.

Use Sources 1, 2 and 3 and your own knowledge.

Do you agree with the view that the perceived failures of the Labour Government were responsible for the victory of the Conservative Party in the 1979 general election?

SOURCE 1

(From the Guardian *newspaper, 5 May 1979)*

After the struggling Labour Government [the Conservatives] offered a policy change. For the State read the individual. 'Substantial' tax cuts. Something done about unions. A blend of traditional Conservative values plus a strong pitch to those simply bored by the long, slow struggle against national economic decline.

SOURCE 2

(From Charles Moore, Margaret Thatcher: The Authorised Biography, *published 2013)*

The Conservative strategy was not to focus on Thatcher as they believed she was 'hard to sell'. The Conservative election campaign of 1979 hit at areas that had traditionally been Labour's strongest points. Unemployment, which had hit 1.5 million in 1977, was an obvious example. An advertising executive invented the slogan 'Labour isn't working'. The poster was heavily featured in newspapers.

SOURCE 3

(From Chris Rowe, Britain, 1929–1998, *published 2004)*

What happened after 1979 tended to distort the truth about the 1979 election. Indeed, a Labour defeat was not a certainty; it was a close-run campaign and Callaghan might have won if he had gone for an election in 1978. Secondly, the Margaret Thatcher of 1979 was not the dominating political figure she later became. Thatcher was an unknown quantity, and, at that time, far from popular, even within her own party.

Thatcher's economic policies

Monetarism, 1980–1983

During her first term Thatcher aimed to reduce inflation. Therefore, Geoffrey Howe's 1980 budget set annual targets for reducing the money supply. His 1981 budget, which raised taxes and cut £3500 million from public spending, was such a radical break with Keynesianism that 364 economists wrote to *The Times* in protest at this new monetarist approach.

Thatcher's monetarist policies succeeded in cutting inflation from 19 per cent in 1979 to 5 per cent in 1983. However, they led to a huge rise in unemployment, from 2,244,000 in 1980 to 3,225,000 in 1983. Additionally, cutting industry subsidies caused many manufacturing businesses to fail and therefore led to a 15 per cent drop in manufacturing output.

Popular capitalism, 1984–1990

Thatcher never abandoned her desire to control inflation. However, in the mid-1980s she did change her approach to achieving this goal. In 1983, the Government recognised that there was no way to accurately measure the money supply and so Thatcher abandoned strict monetarism. The Government's new approach was to use a variety of free market policies, hoping that increased competition would control inflation. These included:

- tax cuts to incentivise hard work
- limiting union power to reduce their ability to force wages up
- reducing welfare provision to cut government spending and ending the **dependency culture** (see page 60)
- privatisation of state-owned industries
- **deregulating** banking, leading to 'easy credit' and an increase in borrowing
- giving council tenants the **'right to buy'** their homes.

Privatisation

Privatisation was a largely popular policy designed to **'roll back the state'**. During the 1980s the Conservatives privatised many state-owned companies.

Year	Company privatised
1980	British Aerospace
1983	British Sugar
1984	British Telecom
1986	British Gas
1987	British Petroleum Rolls Royce
1988	British Steel

The Lawson Boom

The Government claimed its economic policies created a fast rate economic growth in the mid-1980s. During the **Lawson Boom**, the economy achieved high rates of growth and unemployment began to fall.

Year	GDP growth (per cent)	Unemployment
1985	3.6	3,346,000
1986	3.9	3,408,000
1987	4.5	3,297,000
1988	5.2	2,722,000

The Lawson Bust

Nigel Lawson's 1987 and 1988 budgets cut taxes and stimulated consumer spending. Consequently, imports rose and so, during 1989 and 1990, the UK suffered the worst balance of payments crisis ever seen. Increased spending also led to rising inflation, which peaked at 10.9 per cent in 1990.

To combat rising inflation Lawson increased interest rates. This hit everyone who had borrowed money following the deregulation of banking in the mid-1980s, and therefore reduced their spending power. Additionally, high interest rates made borrowing less attractive, which further reduced consumer demand. This fall in demand led to a recession.

Thatcher's economic record

Evidence of success	Evidence of failure
• Between 1979 and 1983, inflation fell dramatically. • GDP grew at record rates during the Lawson Boom. • By 1989, unemployment was lower than it had been in 1979.	• The recession of the early 1980s led to a 15% decline in industrial production between 1979 and 1981. • Lawson's tax cuts created a balance of payments crisis and an economic bust. • The Government's tax take grew from 38.5% of GDP in 1979 to 41% of GDP in 1990. • Inflation increased following the Lawson Boom.

Doing reliability well

Below are a series of definitions listing common reasons why sources are reliable or unreliable, and a source. Under the source, explain why the source is either reliable or unreliable for the purpose stated, justifying your answer by referring to the following definitions.

- **Vested interest**: the source is written so that the writer can protect their power or their financial interests.
- **Second-hand report**: the writer of the source is not an eyewitness, but is relying on someone else's account.
- **Expertise**: the source is written on a subject on which the author (for example, a historian) is an expert.
- **Political bias**: a source is written by a politician and it reflects their political views.
- **Reputation**: a source is written to protect the writer's reputation.

SOURCE 1

(From Chancellor of the Exchequer Nigel Lawson's budget speech, 15 March 1988)

The British economy is stronger than at any time since the war. This has not happened by chance. It has happened because, for almost nine years now, we have followed the right policies and stuck to them. I reaffirm those policies today. In particular, there will be no letting up in our determination to defeat inflation.

> The source is reliable / fairly reliable / fairly unreliable / unreliable as a description of the
> impact of Conservative economic policies in the period 1979–1990 because
>
> _____
>
> _____

 a

Write the question

The sources on this page relate to Conservative economic policy in the period 1979–1989. Write an exam-style part (b) question using the sources.

Use Sources 1, 2 and 3 and your own knowledge. Do you agree with the view that …

_____

_____

Explain your answer using Sources 1, 2 and 3 and your own knowledge.

SOURCE 2

(A transcript of an ITN news report, 1 May 1987)

Mrs Thatcher paid a pre-election visit to the conference of the Confederation of British Industry. The conference delegates and the Prime Minister were cheered by the good trade figures. Speaking to the conference she said: 'People like to feel pride in their country, they like to feel confident in their country, people feel both now.' For the last three months the balance of payments has been in credit. The value of the pound rose against the dollar, and against the index of major currencies.

SOURCE 3

(From a Reuters News report entitled Britain's Conservative Conference Clouded by Economic Troubles, *10 October 1989)*

Britain's Conservative government fought on Tuesday to assert its political authority in the face of a deepening economic crisis. *The Daily Mail,* a prominent pro-government newspaper, called for Chancellor of the Exchequer Nigel Lawson to resign. The paper condemned last week's further rise in interest rates and said ordinary people were paying the price of his 'arrogance and folly'.

But party officials supported the finance minister. Party chairman Kenneth Baker said: 'People are asking, when it comes to the economy have we got it right? I say yes.' Referring to last week's interest rate rise to 15 per cent, a doubling in 18 months, Margaret Thatcher said: 'The interest rate rise was necessary and this government always does what is necessary.'

Union policy

Between 1945 and 1979, governments regularly consulted major unions when making economic policy. Thatcher ended this close relationship and imposed legal limits on union power. She believed that the unions' refusal to allow industry innovation, and their continual demands for higher wages, had contributed to Britain's decline.

Legal measures

By 1984, there were significant legal restrictions on union power.

Act	Measures
1980 Employment Act	Employers were empowered to prosecute unions for taking **secondary action**, including **secondary picketing**.
1982 Employment Act	Union rights to impose a **closed shop** were limited. Union leaders could only do this if they gained the backing of a majority of members in a secret ballot. Sacking workers for not being union members was outlawed. Unions lost the right to insist that employers could only hire unionised workers.
1984 Trade Union Act	Unions were forced to call a secret ballot prior to starting strike action. Strikes were only legal if they were supported by the majority who voted in the ballot.

On top of these legal restrictions, union power was diminished by a 14 per cent fall in union membership between 1979 and 1982.

The miners' strike, 1984–1985

The Conservatives argued that Britain's mines were inefficient and largely unprofitable. Therefore, in 1981, they proposed a series of pit closures. However, following a strike by the National Union of Mineworkers (NUM), the Government backed down.

In 1983, the Government adopted a new strategy. Thatcher appointed Ian MacGregor to make the mining industry profitable again.

A year later, McGregor announced the closure of twenty loss-making pits. In response, on 5 March 1984, Arthur Scargill called a strike, although he did not ballot the whole union and therefore Thatcher argued that the strike was illegal.

During the strike there were several clashes between miners and the police. One of the most famous, the 'Battle of Orgreave' on 18 June 1984, was a confrontation between up to 8000 police officers and 6000 striking miners.

The end of the strike

Thatcher was determined to win the battle with the miners. She did not want to repeat Heath's mistakes and allow the strike to bring down her Government (see page 42). Her strategy was to refuse to give in and wait for the miners to back down. After 362 days the NUM were forced to end the strike. Thatcher's strategy had worked for the following reasons.

- The Government was able to minimise the effects of the strike because it had increased the stockpile of coal, and spent £20 million per week on oil, an alternative to coal.
- The Nottinghamshire Miners' Association split away from the NUM, creating the Union of Democratic Mineworkers (UDM). UDM disagreed with the strike and continued working.
- The NUM ran out of money and could no longer support striking workers.

Government victory

The Government's victory led to the following changes in the coal industry.

- Forty-two pits were closed.
- The number of miners fell from 181,000 to 108,000.
- Productivity rose. In 1984, miners produced an average of 2.59 tonnes per shift. By 1987, this had risen to 3.96 tonnes.

More generally, the victory showed that Thatcher's union laws, unlike Heath's Industrial Relations Act (see page 42), were successful. For many Conservatives, Thatcher's victory symbolised the 'taming' of the unions.

Spot the mistake

Below are a sample exam-style part (a) question and a paragraph written in answer to this question. Why does this paragraph not get into Level 4? Once you have identified the mistake, rewrite the paragraph so that it displays the qualities of Level 4. The mark scheme on page 78 will help you.

Study Sources 1, 2 and 3. How far do the sources agree that Margaret Thatcher was willing to compromise with the miners during the miners' strike of 1984–1985?

Sources 1 and 3 disagree with Source 2 that Margaret Thatcher was willing to compromise with the miners. Source 1 states that 'Thatcher wanted to crush the miners', suggesting that Thatcher was not willing to compromise with them. Source 3 supports this interpretation, suggesting that the Conservative Government viewed the miners as 'scum', and stating 'Who wants compromise? — not Thatcher'. However, the political bias of both sources may help to explain why they present contrasting interpretations to Source 2. Source 1 is from the recollections of a miner who was involved in the strike and Source 3 is written by a member of the Labour Party. In this sense, both authors are likely to view Thatcher's actions and motivations negatively.

SOURCE 1

(From the recollections of Ken Radford, a former miner present at the Battle of Orgreave in 1984)
Thatcher wanted to crush the miners. That was her goal, that's all she wanted. That day at Orgreave was planned. They cordoned us off, there were more police than normal. They blocked off the gates down at the bottom. All of a sudden … horses came and they just charged. I don't know how many were injured, there were a lot of lads just covered in blood.

SOURCE 2

(From the recollections of Phillip Oppenheim, Conservative MP for the Amber Valley, 1983–1997)
The Thatcher government was never certain of victory and would have settled the strike on reasonable terms, which were never on offer. In countless meetings with Mrs Thatcher at the time of the strike, I never heard the language of war or revenge, only regret at the dispute and respect for miners and their communities.

SOURCE 3

(From the diary of Stuart Smith, 1 October 1984. Smith was a member of the Labour Party.)
If they imprison Scargill it will lead to riot. But then that is just what the Tory government wants – an image of saving the nation from 'the scum'. Who wants compromise? – not Thatcher.

 Spot the inference

High level answers avoid summarising or paraphrasing the sources, and instead make inferences from the sources. Read Source 2 above and decide which of the statements:
- make inferences from the source (I)
- summarise the source (S)
- paraphrase the source (P)
- cannot be justified from the source (X)

Statement	I	P	S	X
The miners were not willing to compromise with the Government.				
The Conservative Government was willing to settle the strike on terms that were reasonable.				
The Conservative Government was willing to compromise to end the strike.				
Margaret Thatcher regretted having to order the closure of the mines.				

Welfare reform

Welfare and the New Right

Thatcher's welfare policies influenced the New Right. Specifically, New Right thinkers argued that high levels of welfare spending were a problem.

- Welfare spending had an **opportunity cost**: money spent on welfare could not be invested in industry. Therefore, welfare spending 'crowded out' private spending and denied industry the opportunity to grow.
- High levels of welfare created a 'dependency culture' in which people relied on welfare payment rather than earning their own money.

Despite these arguments, Thatcher was relatively slow to reform welfare and never succeeded in cutting the Government's welfare budget.

Social security

Social security payments increased significantly due to the rise in unemployment in the early 1980s. To stop payments rising, the Government introduced a series of reforms in the 1986 Social Security Act.

Social Security Act (1986)

The Act:

- simplified the social security system and stopped overlapping benefits
- replaced payments for those with emergency needs with loans
- required recipients of social security to pay 20 per cent of the **rates**.

Pensions

Conservative policy attempted to halt the growth of spending on pensions. Since 1945, the basic state pension had been **uprated** in line with the growth in earnings. From 1982, the Government changed this so that pensions were uprated in line with price inflation. This made the rate of increase much smaller.

From 1986, the Government encouraged people to opt out of **SERPS** and find private pension providers. When people opted out the Government gave them a lump sum that could be invested with a private pension company.

Education

The education budget was cut by 70 per cent between 1979 and 1983. Major reform was introduced by the 1988 Education Reform Act. This introduced the National Curriculum, including standardised tests for children aged seven, eleven and fourteen. The Government published the test results in the form of league tables. Ministers argued this would allow parents to see how well schools were performing, and enable parents to send their children to the best schools. The Government claimed that introducing competition into education would improve educational standards.

The Act also allowed schools to opt out of local authority control to allow schools to get money directly from central government and manage their own budgets. It was hoped that this would encourage good schools to expand.

Health

In **absolute terms** the NHS budget rose considerably from £7.5 billion in 1979 to £29 billion in 1990. However, in **real terms** NHS budgets barely increased. To help control costs the Government introduced 'compulsory competitive purchasing' in 1983. This meant that hospitals were required to buy in services such as cleaning and catering from private companies.

By 1988, NHS underfunding was becoming headline news. Thatcher responded by announcing radical reform. The 1988 Health **White Paper** proposed creating an internal market in the NHS. This was achieved in the 1990 National Health Service and Community Care Act.

- Health Authorities would no longer manage local hospitals. They would purchase services from hospitals instead.
- Hospitals would be responsible for their own budgets.
- Hospitals would compete for Health Authority contracts.
- Successful hospitals could expand their services. Failing hospitals would close.

Ministers claimed that the internal market would make the NHS more efficient.

Linking sources

Below are a sample exam-style part (a) question and the three sources referred to in the question. In one colour, draw links between the sources to show ways in which they agree about reactions to the introduction of the National Curriculum in 1988. In another colour, draw links between the sources to show ways in which they disagree.

Study Sources 1, 2 and 3. How far do the sources suggest that the National Curriculum of 1988 received widespread support within Britain?

SOURCE 1

(From New Scientist magazine, 8 September 1988)

Teachers will not be trained in the new curriculum until after they begin teaching it next year. The National Union of Teachers said that the effect of rushing through these plans in this way would be 'very damaging' to the education of children. 'Such a lot is being asked of teachers in such a short space of time. Teachers need to be confident with the material they teach.'

However, Cecily Gale, a biology teacher, stressed that most teachers she knew did not object to the proposals. 'We are happy to put them into effect if given the training, support and time,' she said.

SOURCE 2

(From a speech by Derek Fatchett, Labour MP for Leeds, 16 January 1989)

We have had differences with Conservative MPs about the detail of the national curriculum, but they will recall that at no stage did we vote against the principle of the national curriculum. The Secretary of State even criticised us for not putting up sufficient opposition to the introduction of the national curriculum.

SOURCE 3

(From a speech by Timothy Devlin, Conservative MP for Stockton South, 28 February 1989)

The lack of correspondence from the people of Cleveland shows that the overwhelming majority are very happy with the new arrangements for higher standards introduced through the national curriculum. It will receive a general welcome throughout the county, contrary to the allegations of the local Labour Party.

 Explain the difference (a)

Sources 2 and 3 above give different accounts of the impact of the reaction of the Labour Party to the National Curriculum of 1988. List the ways in which the sources differ. Explain the differences between the sources using the provenance and the content of the sources. The provenance appears at the top of the sources in brackets.

Thatcher's critics

Revised

The 'Thatcher Revolution' was highly controversial and faced criticism from across the political spectrum.

Rivalries within the Conservative Party

'Wets' and 'dries'

Initially, Thatcher's Cabinet included many Conservatives who had supported Heath. These **'wets'**, including Francis Pym, Jim Prior and Peter Carrington, persuaded Thatcher to maintain public spending in the first year of her Government.

However, Thatcher refused to give up on monetarism. She famously rejected a U-turn at the 1980 Conservative Party Conference, telling her critics, 'the lady's not for turning'. By 1981, she was able to push through a radical monetarist budget (see page 56). Britain's victory in the 1982 **Falklands War** against Argentina, and Thatcher's landslide election victory in 1983, strengthened her position. Consequently, by 1984, Pym, Prior and Carrington had all lost their Cabinet posts.

Following the 1983 election, Thatcher included an increasing number of Thatcherite **'dries'** in senior Cabinet positions, such as Nigel Lawson and Leon Brittan.

Michael Heseltine

Michael Heseltine was associated with Cabinet 'wets'. Following the **Brixton and Toxteth riots** of 1981 he argued that the Government should do more to promote growth in underprivileged areas. He used his power as Secretary of State for the Environment to establish Enterprise Zones and Development Corporations to help regenerate urban areas. Thatcher viewed these initiatives as useful publicity campaigns. By contrast, Heseltine argued that they showed government intervention was still necessary.

Thatcher and Heseltine were also divided on the issues of Britain's relationship with Europe. This difference came to a head during the Westland affair of 1986. The Cabinet was split over the future of Westland Helicopters, a struggling British company. Heseltine argued that Westland Helicopters should join a European consortium. Leon Brittan argued that the American company Sikorski should take over Westland. Thatcher backed Brittan's American takeover. As a result Heseltine resigned from the Cabinet, criticising Thatcher's policies and her **authoritarian** leadership style.

Left-wing critics

For much of the early 1980s the Labour Party was so divided that the party's leadership offered little effective resistance to Thatcherism. However, the Labour-led Greater London Council (GLC) offered a radical alternative. Ken Livingstone, the GLC's leader, described this as 'urban socialism'. He argued that Thatcher was marginalising minority groups, ignoring environmental issues and risking nuclear war. Livingstone used GLC money to give grants to radical groups such as the **Race Today Collective**, and raised rates to lower bus fares and to set up the GLC Ecological Gardens on the South Bank of the Thames. He even used government money set aside for preparing for a nuclear war to fund an anti-nuclear campaign. Thatcher's response was to cap GLC spending and pass a law abolishing the GLC.

The SDP/Liberal Alliance

Thatcher also faced opposition from the SDP/Liberal Alliance. Following the election of a left-wing Labour leader in 1980, a group of Labour MPs left the party to set up the Social Democratic Party (SDP). The SDP formed an alliance with the Liberal Party. Together, the SDP and Liberals argued that they represented a moderate alternative to the increasingly extreme Conservative and Labour Parties. The SDP/Liberal Alliance argued that constitutional change was needed for:

- **devolution** in Scotland and Wales
- **proportional representation**
- freedom of information
- a democratic alternative to the House of Lords.

Complete the table

Use the information on the opposite page to add detail to the table below.

	Critics	Nature of criticism	Impact of criticism
Within the Conservative Party	'Wets'		
	Michael Heseltine		
Outside the conservative Party	Left-wing critics		
	SDP/Liberal Alliance		

Support or challenge?

Below is a sample exam-style part (b) question which asks you how far the sources agree with a specific statement. Below this are the three sources which give information relevant to the question. Identify whether the sources support, mainly support, mainly challenge, or challenge the statement in the question and then give reasons for your answer.

Use Sources 1, 2 and 3 and your own knowledge. Do you agree with the view that criticism of Thatcher's policies was a threat to Conservative Government in the period 1979–1986?

SOURCE 1

(From the recollections of David Owen. Owen was leader of the SDP from 1983–1987 and 1988–1990)

Thatcher would not have remained Prime Minister if it were not for the Falklands War. It is easy to forget that in the first two weeks of 1982 her government was in trouble. Two opinion polls put the SDP–Liberal Alliance ahead at 34% and 36% respectively, with the Tories coming second and third respectively.

> This source supports / mainly supports / mainly challenges / challenges the view that criticism of Thatcher's policies was a threat to the Conservative Government in the period 1979–1986 because
>
> _____
>
> _____

SOURCE 2

(From Michael Lynch, Britain 1945–2007, *published 2008)*

Nobody came out of the Westland affair with credit. Critics suggested that the whole thing showed up the unattractive aspects of Mrs Thatcher's government. However, the internal squabble over Westland did not greatly harm the government's standing with the voters. The year 1987 witnessed Mrs Thatcher's third consecutive electoral victory.

> This source supports / mainly supports / mainly challenges / challenges the view that criticism of Thatcher's policies was a threat to the Conservative Government in the period 1979–1986 because
>
> _____
>
> _____

SOURCE 3

(From Earl Aaron Reitan, The Thatcher Revolution, *published 2003)*

The GLC caused problems for Thatcher. From 1981 to 1986 Ken Livingstone increased GLC expenditures by 170 per cent. He claimed to be creating 'urban socialism' as an alternative to Thatcherism. He posted a banner listing the figures for unemployment.

Thatcher's answer to this was a demonstration of raw power. In 1985, the Thatcher ministry proposed abolition of eighteen urban councils. Labour controlled all but two. The list included the GLC.

> This source supports / mainly supports / mainly challenges / challenges the view that criticism of Thatcher's policies was a threat to the Conservative Government in the period 1979–1986 because
>
> _____
>
> _____

Local government and the poll tax

Thatcher was determined to 'roll back the state'. This included reducing the role of local government.

Housing

Housing was one area where the Government succeeded in reducing spending and shifting the balance away from the state towards the free market. Indeed, the Conservative housing budget was 40 per cent lower in 1983 than in 1979.

The 1980 Housing Act gave council tenants the 'right to buy' their homes. Additionally, council houses were sold at a discount of between 30 per cent and 50 per cent of the market value. The policy was extremely popular; in 1982 alone, 250,000 council houses were sold as part of the scheme.

The Community Charge

Replacing the rates

The Community Charge was introduced to reform local government. It replaced the rates as the tax which funded local government. It was widely agreed that the rates were unfair. The rates were based on the value of property, therefore a household consisting of a single income earner would pay the same as a household of multiple income earners, as long as their houses were the same value.

The Adam Smith Institute, a right-wing 'think tank' advising the Government on economic policy, recommended replacing the rates with a flat rate charge. This meant that all adults in a local area would pay the same local tax. Thatcher believed that this would be a fairer system. Additionally, she believed that having a tax all adults were obliged to pay would make local government more accountable, as all taxpayers would have an interest in keeping the cost of local government as low as possible. Indeed, Thatcher hoped that the introduction of the new tax would persuade many to vote against Labour councils, which tended to set higher taxes than Conservative councils.

The Local Government Finance Act 1988 introduced the Community Charge. It was a flat rate tax for all working people in a specific district. Students and the unemployed were only required to pay twenty per cent of the regular amount.

Backlash

The community charge, or poll tax, proved to be extremely unpopular. Opponents argued that it was unfair as all working people were required to pay the same amount, regardless of their earnings. Consequently, it would hit the poor much harder than the rich.

The All Britain Anti-Poll Tax Federation ('the Fed') organised a non-payment campaign. Similarly, in Scotland, the Scottish National Party (SNP) organised the 'Can't pay, won't pay' campaign. These campaigns were extremely successful: of the 38 million who required to pay, 18 million refused. As a result the Community Charge was two and a half times more expensive to collect than the rates.

The Fed also organised mass demonstrations against the new tax. On 31 March 1990, 50,000 marched in Glasgow and 200,000 marched in London. The latter demonstration turned into a full scale riot.

Thatcher's response

Following the poll tax riots, Thatcher's Cabinet colleagues urged her to rethink. Remarkably, Thatcher refused to back down. For many Conservative MPs Thatcher's refusal to compromise showed that she was no longer in touch with the views of the British people.

RAG – Rate the timeline

Below are a sample exam-style question and a timeline. Read the question, study the timeline and, using three coloured pens, put a red, amber or green star next to the events to show:

● **Red:** Events and policies that have no relevance to the question

● **Amber:** Events and policies that have some significance to the question

● **Green:** Events and policies that are directly relevant to the question

1) Do you agree with the view that, in the years 1979–1990, the Conservative Government's failures outweighed its successes?

Now repeat the activity with the following questions:

2) Do you agree with the view that Margaret Thatcher's time as Prime Minister ended the post-war consensus in British politics?

3) Do you agree with the view that the introduction of the poll tax was the main reason for the downfall of Margaret Thatcher in 1990?

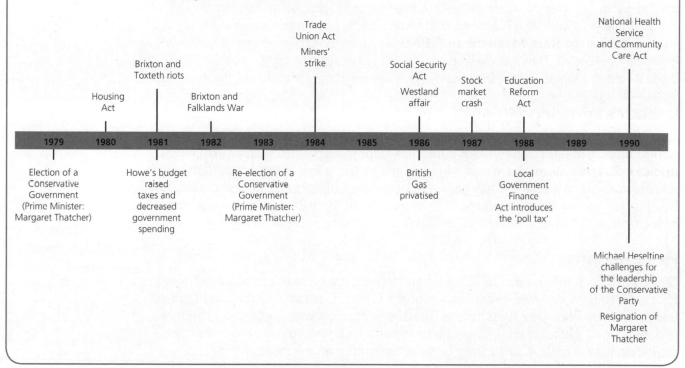

Recommended reading

Below is a list of suggested further reading on this topic.

● *Britain 1945–2007*, pages 116–62, Michael Lynch (2008)

● *Thatcher,* Chapters 5 and 6, Clare Beckett (2006)

● *Hope and Glory: Britain 1900–2000,* Chapter 11, Peter Clark (2004)

Thatcher's fall

Revised

Thatcher's last years were increasingly troubled. Economic problems, splits over Europe, the poll tax and the revival of the Labour Party all played a part in her downfall.

Economic problems

Thatcher's position was weakened by the return of economic problems. On Black Monday, 19 October 1987, Britain suffered a stock market crash which wiped £102 million from the value of British shares. Following the crash, Britain's economic problems worsened as the Lawson Boom turned to bust (see page 56).

Europe

Britain's relationship with Europe was another problem. Europe became a key issue in the late 1980s due to Lawson's economic policy. His solution to rising inflation was to **peg** the value of the pound to the value of the **Deutschmark**. Lawson argued that ensuring that the pound was worth approximately 2.95DM would keep Britain competitive internationally. Lawson and Howe wanted to take this policy further and take Britain into the **Exchange Rate Mechanism (ERM)**, a system that linked the value of major European currencies. Thatcher was reluctant to do so because the creation of the ERM was the first step to a single European currency. This disagreement created a split in the Cabinet.

Labour's growing strength

Labour's growing popularity was a further reason for Thatcher's troubles. Labour Leader Neil Kinnock had reformed the party, dropping unpopular policies such as **unilateral nuclear disarmament** and accepting many of Thatcher's free market ideas. Labour was also popular because of Thatcher's refusal to compromise over the poll tax (see page 64). The party's popularity, seen too in its victory in the 1989 European election, raised concerns that Thatcher could no longer guarantee electoral success for the Conservatives.

Resignations

Disagreements over Britain's ERM membership led Lawson to resign as Chancellor in 1989. His resignation was embarrassing for the Government as Thatcher and Lawson had once been allies. The weakness of Thatcher's position was exposed by changes in the Cabinet. Thatcher felt compelled to appoint well-known 'wets' to important positions, for example, Chris Patten became Environment Secretary in 1989.

Sir Anthony Meyer's 1989 leadership challenge also indicated that Thatcher's post was under attack. Meyer criticised the poll tax and Thatcher's growing **Euroscepticism**. It was assumed that Meyer was acting as a 'stalking horse': opening up a challenge to allow other potential challengers to step forward, if Thatcher's position proved weak. However, Thatcher gained the support of 84 per cent of Conservative MPs and therefore continued as leader.

Geoffrey Howe's resignation in November 1990 was the short-term cause of Thatcher's fall. Howe, like Lawson and Meyer, disliked Thatcher's Euroscepticism and her authoritarian style. His resignation speech, which was highly critical of Thatcher's policy regarding the ERM, further damaged her reputation.

The 1990 leadership contest

Following Howe's resignation, Heseltine announced he would challenge Thatcher for the leadership. Unlike Meyer, Heseltine was a serious candidate. However, Heseltine only gained 40 per cent of the vote. Even so, Thatcher's victory was not large enough to end the contest. Thatcher initially declared that she would fight on, but meetings with her Cabinet persuaded her that she could not win. She withdrew from the race and resigned as Prime Minister at the end of November 1990.

Develop the detail

Below are a sample exam-style part (b) question and a paragraph written in answer to this question. The question refers to the sources on this page. The paragraph contains a limited amount of own knowledge. Annotate the paragraph to add additional own knowledge to the answer.

Use Sources 1, 2 and 3 and your own knowledge. Do you agree with the view that the main reason for Margaret Thatcher's downfall was the resignation of Geoffrey Howe?

In addition to the resignation of Geoffrey Howe, divisions over Conservative policies were responsible for the downfall of Margaret Thatcher. First, the introduction of the poll tax was unpopular with both the public and members of the Conservative Government. In Source 3, Geoffrey Howe recalls that 'her commitment to the poll tax was almost certainly taking us to disaster'. Her views on Europe also faced opposition within the Conservative Party. Source 1 refers to 'repeated rows over monetary union with Britain's European partners'. In addition, Source 2 states that '[Howe] said that his loyalty to Mrs Thatcher conflicted with what he perceived "to be the best interests of the nation"'. Thatcher's reluctance to develop a closer relationship with Europe created a divide within her Cabinet. In this way, divisions over the poll tax and Europe isolated Thatcher within her Government.

SOURCE 1

(From Kenneth O. Morgan, Twentieth-Century Britain, *published 2000)*

Thatcher herself became increasingly unpopular. Her intensely personal, domineering style of leadership now seemed a liability. Her reputation for 'strength' in foreign affairs, dating from the Falklands War, also seemed less credible, especially with repeated rows over monetary union with Britain's European partners. At the same time, the Labour Party, led by Neil Kinnock, became more electable.

SOURCE 2

(From Terry Warner, Margaret Thatcher, *published 2012)*

In the end, it wasn't angry protestors that finished off Mrs Thatcher. It was Geoffrey Howe's resignation speech, to a packed House of Commons, that dealt the fatal blow. He said that his loyalty to Mrs Thatcher conflicted with what he perceived 'to be the best interests of the nation'. That Howe could say this about the woman he had supported for over a decade and who he knew better than most signalled to her chief opponents that she was vulnerable. Heseltine saw his moment and promptly challenged for the leadership of the Conservative Party.

SOURCE 3

(From the recollections of Geoffrey Howe, published in the Guardian, *8 April 2013)*

My resignation speech, in November 1990, was made with genuine regret. I have often said that I was seeking a change in policy not a change in prime minister. But I suppose I was beginning to realise that that was an unlikely outcome, just as others were recognising that her commitment to the poll tax was almost certainly taking us to disaster.

Section 4: Exam focus

On pages 69–71 are sample answers to the exam-style questions on this page. Read the answers and the examiner comments around them.

a) Study Sources 1, 2 and 3.

How far do the sources suggest that Margaret Thatcher was a divisive Prime Minister? Explain your answer using the evidence of Sources 1, 2 and 3. **(20 marks)**

b) Use Sources 4, 5 and 6 and your own knowledge.

Do you agree with the view that Conservative economic policy was unsuccessful in the period 1979–1990? Explain your answer using Sources 4, 5 and 6 and your own knowledge. **(40 marks)**

SOURCE 1

(From an interview with Margaret Thatcher as she arrived at 10 Downing Street on her first day as Prime Minister)

Her Majesty the Queen has asked me to form a new government, and I have accepted. It is, of course, the greatest honour that can come to any citizen in a democracy. I will strive unceasingly to try to fulfil the trust and confidence that the British people have placed in me, and the things in which I believe.

'Where there is discord, may we bring harmony. Where there is error, may we bring truth. Where there is doubt, may we bring faith. And where there is despair, may we bring hope.'

SOURCE 2

(Mike Bryant, speaking in 2013, recalls his impressions of Margaret Thatcher. Bryant was a sixth form student in Manchester at the time of Margaret Thatcher's resignation in 1990)

The thing I remember most about Thatcher is how divisive she was. I came from a middle-class radical family. We went on CND marches and attended Labour Party rallies. We had a satirical picture of Thatcher on our kitchen wall! What I remember was during the miners' strike you either agreed with her or you didn't; there was no real debate. Looking back, I didn't have much of an idea about the differences of opinion within the Tory Party. I knew that there was a person called Margaret Thatcher and that we disagreed with her. Things were very polarised.

SOURCE 3

(From the Boston Globe's *article 'The Thatcher Decade of Discontent', 28 November 1990)*

Regarding Margaret Thatcher, a few truths have been lost in the fog surrounding her resignation. Cruelty is not toughness, merely cruelty; failure is not boldness, merely failure; obstinacy is not conviction, merely obstinacy. According to some, she represents Britain's bold effort to shake off its post-war decline and strive again to be great. Baloney. In 11 years, she never could persuade a majority of her country's voters to support her, and thus her policies, for the simple reason that she and her policies did more harm than good.

SOURCE 4

(From 'The London Year in Review', published in the financial magazine the International Trader, *31 December 1990)*

The year 1990 in London was one to forget. The stock market fell some 10%. Margaret Thatcher fell from office, and the British economy was beset by high inflation, crippling interest rates and a persistent balance of payments deficit. Some companies still made money. Shares in Water, which was privatized a year ago, rose some 9%. Amstrad, a computer company, was a big loser in 1989, its share price falling 77%.

SOURCE 5

(From Roger Lloyd-Jones, Myrddin John Lewis and Merv J. Lewis, British Industrial Capitalism Since the Industrial Revolution, *published 1998)*

For those on the right of the political spectrum the 1980s witnessed a renaissance for the British economy. Even historians, not fully convinced of an 'economic miracle', have nonetheless given considerable support to the notion that the British economy returned to a path of growth allowing Britain to catch up with the economies that overtook during the 1950s and 1960s.

SOURCE 6

(From Maurice Mullard, Policy-Making in Britain, *published 2013)*

Despite the short boom of 1987 unemployment never fell below 2 million during the Thatcher years. This is a stark contrast to the 1950s and 1960s when unemployment peaked at 250,000. It is, nonetheless, true that trade union militancy was on the decline during the 1980s as the number of strikes fell to the levels of the 1950s.

a) Study Sources 1, 2 and 3.

How far do the sources suggest that Margaret Thatcher was a divisive Prime Minister? Explain your answer using the evidence of Sources 1, 2 and 3. **(20 marks)**

Sources 2 and 3 clearly indicate that Margaret Thatcher was a greatly divisive Prime Minister. However, Source 1 indicates that Thatcher was trying to heal and unite the nation rather than cause greater division.

Source 2 is clear: 'The thing I remember most about Thatcher is how divisive she was.' This is supported by Source 3 which argues that 'she never could persuade a majority of her country's voters to support her'. Source 2 illustrates just how opposed some British people were to Thatcher's policies. 'We had a satirical picture of Thatcher on our kitchen wall!' Source 2 is clearly politically biased against Thatcher. Source 2 also alludes to the fact that even the Conservative Party was divided during Thatcher's time in office, noting 'differences of opinion within the Tory Party'. However, neither Source 2 nor Source 3 support the view that dislike of Thatcher was widespread. Bryant, who is quoted in the source, acknowledges that he 'came from a middle-class radical family. We went on CND marches and attended Labour Party rallies.' Therefore he is unrepresentative of the country as a whole. Equally, Source 3's statement that the majority never voted for Thatcher is less convincing due to the fact the almost no post-war government gained a majority of support at election time. Therefore, although Source 2 clearly indicates that there were some who strongly opposed Thatcher, neither source demonstrates that this strength of feeling was widespread enough to justify the conclusion that Thatcher was a divisive Prime Minister. Nonetheless, Source 1 does indicate that Thatcher was prepared to be divisive. She states, 'I will strive unceasingly to try to fulfil the trust and confidence that the British people have placed in me, and the things in which I believe.' The last part of the sentence indicates that she would govern as a conviction politician. Source 3 supports this noting that 'obstinacy is not conviction, merely obstinacy'. Indeed, Thatcher's commitment to governing from her own conviction is the best evidence that the sources provide for her as a divisive leader.

Source 1, by contrast, indicates that Thatcher intended to be a figure of unity. In her first speech as Prime Minister she appeals to values that unite the vast majority of British people such as 'democracy'. Equally, she pledges to 'fulfil the trust and confidence that the British people have placed in me' indicating that she wants to serve the whole nation. However, Thatcher was speaking soon after the 'winter of discontent' when the country was far from united. Therefore, she had good political reasons to over-emphasise her commitment to unity. Additionally, as the speech was given in 1979, it tells us very little about how she actually governed; therefore it is only of limited usefulness when considering the question.

In conclusion, it is clear from Source 1 that Thatcher was a 'conviction politician'. Source 3 shows that over the next eleven years this led to division. Source 2 is useful for indicating just how far some groups opposed Thatcher, but it cannot tell us how far the nation as a whole viewed Thatcher as a divisive Prime Minister.

20/20

This essay gets a mark in Level 4 because it contains a detailed comparison of the sources, with a strong focus on the question. What is more, the second paragraph contains a sophisticated treatment of the provenance of the sources, distinguishing between Source 2's strength of feeling and the extent to which it is representative of broader opinion.

The introduction answers the question with a summary of the sources. Nonetheless, it does not fully reflect the argument that emerges from the rest of the essay.

This paragraph immediately highlights a similarity between Sources 2 and 3, and therefore begins the essay with clear comparison.

The candidate considers the provenance of Source 2 in order to evaluate how far it provides evidence that Thatcher was a divisive figure.

The candidate also considers the strength of the argument made by Source 3 by referring to historical context.

This paragraph also considers the extent to which Source 1 is evidence that Thatcher wanted national unity by relating it to its context.

The conclusion evaluates the extent to which Thatcher was a divisive leader by referring back to the provenance discussed earlier in the essay.

b) Use Sources 4, 5 and 6 and your own knowledge.

Do you agree with the view that Conservative economic policy was unsuccessful in the period 1979–1990? Explain your answer using Sources 4, 5 and 6 and your own knowledge. **(40 marks)**

Conservative economic policy in the period 1979–1990 was partly successful. Generally, the Government was successful at keeping inflation low, at tackling 'trade union militancy' (Source 6), and privatisation brought profitable companies into the private sector (Source 5). However, the Government never managed to achieve sustained growth, nor did it solve the problem of unemployment (Source 6).

> The essay begins by setting out the different aspects of Conservative economic policy, and makes an initial judgement about how far each area was a success.

Source 5 argues that 'those on the right' see 'the 1980s witnessed a renaissance for the British economy'. There is some evidence to support this view. Thatcher's prime economic objective was cutting inflation and the Government succeeded in reducing inflation from nineteen per cent in 1979 to five per cent in 1983. Even the 'high inflation' that returned to the economy in 1990 was lower than the inflation of 1979. Equally, privatisation was popular with many on the right, who believed that the private sector was more efficient than the public sector and should therefore run business. Between 1980 and 1989 the Government privatised British Aerospace, British Sugar, British Telecom, British Gas, British Petroleum, Rolls Royce, British Steel and the water companies. Low inflation, low taxes and easy credit led to 'the short boom of 1987' (Source 6). What is more, as Source 4 shows, shares in some of the privatised companies, such as water, were still rising despite the stock market crash of 1989. In this way, it is clear that there were some successes as inflation was low compared to 1989 and because privatisation was popular and often profitable. Therefore, there is some justice in Source 5's claim that under Thatcher 'the British economy returned to a path of growth allowing Britain to catch up with the economies that overtook during the 1950s and 1960s'.

> The paragraph evaluates the argument that Conservative economic policy was successful.

> This paragraph includes arguments and evidence from all three of the sources, integrating them with detailed own knowledge.

However, there were significant economic problems during the period 1979–1990. Source 6 argues that the key problem was that 'unemployment never fell below 2 million during the Thatcher years'. Indeed, as inflation dropped from 1979 to 1983, unemployment rose from 1,464,000 in 1979 to 3,225,000 in 1983. Source 6 argues that these figures were extremely high, particularly compared to the '1950s and 1960s when unemployment peaked at 250,000'. However, unlike most post-war governments, the Thatcher Government was not committed to full employment. Rather, its prime economic goals were to reduce inflation and to end trade union militancy. Indeed, high levels of unemployment were necessary to achieve both of these goals. Reducing government spending helped control inflation, but led to much higher unemployment, and higher unemployment meant that workers were less likely to strike for fear of losing their jobs. Therefore, although Source 6 is correct that unemployment was a major problem in the period 1979–1990, it was not an economic failure in Thatcher's view because it was a price worth paying to achieve her other goals.

> This paragraph provides a balance to the previous paragraph by focusing on the economic problems that persisted through Thatcher's rule.

> The paragraph considers the extent to which high unemployment is evidence of failure, by linking it to the Government's goals.

Nonetheless, Sources 4 and 6 argue that there were continuing economic problems. Source 4 argues that at the end of the 1980s there was a return to economic trouble. In 1990, 'the stock market fell some 10%' and big businesses such as Amstrad lost 77 per cent of their value. Taken together, Sources 4 and 6 show that following the 'short boom of 1987' there was a crash leading to 'high inflation, crippling interest rates and a persistent balance of payments deficit'. Unlike unemployment these were economic problems that Thatcher was very concerned about. What is more, they were caused in part by the deregulation of credit. Easy credit created an unsustainable boom, leading to a bust in 1989.

Having argued that high unemployment was not a sign of economic failure because the Thatcher Government was not committed to the goal of full employment, this paragraph examines evidence that the Thatcher Government failed to achieve its explicit economic goals.

Overall, Conservative economic policy was only partly unsuccessful in the period 1979–1990 because it did succeed in two of its major objectives. First, it brought down inflation, at least until 1989. Secondly, it ended trade union militancy, 'as the number of strikes fell to the levels of the 1950s' (Source 6). In so doing Conservative economic policy led to high, but acceptable levels of unemployment to Thatcher and her chancellors. However, in other ways Conservative economic policy failed. Specifically, the deregulation of credit led to a short lived boom followed by a bust in 1989.

The conclusion makes an overall judgement, summarising the argument of the rest of the essay.

35/40

This response is strong in terms of own knowledge and the use of the source material. In terms of the use of own knowledge, the essay receives a mark in Level 4 due to the strong focus on the question, the accuracy and detail of the supporting evidence, and the fact that it integrates the sources with own knowledge to reach a fully justified conclusion. The use of the sources is also strong as throughout the essay they help support the conclusions reached. The essay does not get full marks as it only considers three factors.

What makes a good answer?

You have now considered four sample A-grade exam responses. Use the examples of Part (a) and Part (b) essays contained in the four Exam Focus sections to make two bullet-pointed lists of the characteristics of A-grade Part (a) and Part (b) essays. Use these lists when planning and writing your own practice exam essays.

Timeline

1942	Beveridge Report
1944	Education Act (Butler Act)
1945	End of Second World War
	Election of Labour Government (Prime Minister: Clement Attlee)
1946	Nationalisation of the Bank of England, the coal industry
	Anglo-American Loan
	Start of bread rationing
	National Insurance Act
	National Health Service Act
1947	School leaving age increased to 15
	Dollar crisis
	Nationalisation of transport and electricity
1948	Marshall Aid
	End of bread rationing
1949	Nationalisation of iron and steel industries
1950	Re-election of Labour Government (Prime Minister: Clement Attlee)
	Start of Korean War
1951	Election of Conservative Government (Prime Minister: Winston Churchill)
1955	Resignation of Winston Churchill; Anthony Eden becomes Prime Minister
	Re-election of a Conservative Government (Prime Minister: Anthony Eden)
1956	Suez Crisis
1957	Resignation of Anthony Eden; Harold Macmillan becomes Prime Minister
1959	Re-election of a Conservative Government (Prime Minister: Harold Macmillan)
1962	Establishment of 'Neddy' and 'Nicky'
1963	Profumo Affair
	Resignation of Harold Macmillan; Alec Douglas-Home becomes Prime Minister
1964	Election of a Labour Government (Prime Minister: Harold Wilson)
1965	Comprehensive education system introduced
	National Board for Prices and Incomes set up
1966	Re-election of a Labour Government (Prime Minister: Harold Wilson)
1967	Sexual Offences Act
	Abortion Act
	Family Planning Act
	Devaluation of the pound
1969	*In Place of Strife* published
	Open University established
1970	Election of a Conservative Government (Prime Minister: Edward Heath)
1971	Industrial Relations Act
	Milk Act
1972	Miners' strike

1973	Britain joins the EEC
	National Health Service Reorganisation Act
	School leaving age increased to 16
	OPEC crisis
1974	Three-day week introduced
	Miners' strike
	Election of a hung parliament (Prime Minister: Harold Wilson)
	Industrial Relations Act abolished
	Election of a Labour Government (Prime Minister: Harold Wilson)
1976	Resignation of Harold Wilson; James Callaghan becomes Prime Minister
	Healey's budget decreases government spending
	Education Act
	IMF loan agreed
1977	Lib–Lab Pact agreed
1978	Lib–Lab Pact ends
1979	Winter of Discontent
	Election of a Conservative Government (Prime Minister: Margaret Thatcher)
1980	Housing Act
1981	Creation of Social Democratic Party (SDP)
	Brixton and Toxteth riots
1982	Falklands War
	Employment Act
1983	Re-election of a Conservative Government (Prime Minister: Margaret Thatcher)
1984	Beginning of the miners' strike
	Trade Union Act
1985	End of the miners' strike
1986	Westland affair
	GLC abolished
	British Gas privatised
1987	Re-election of a Conservative Government (Prime Minister: Margaret Thatcher)
	Stock market crash
1988	Education Reform Act
	British steel privatised
	Local Government Finance Act introduces the poll tax
1989	Balance of payments crisis
	Resignation of Nigel Lawson
	Anthony Meyer challenges for the leadership of the Conservative Party
1990	National Health Service and Community Care Act
	Resignation of Geoffrey Howe
	Michael Heseltine challenges for the leadership of the Conservative Party
	Resignation of Margaret Thatcher

Glossary

'A land fit for heroes' A slogan used by the Liberal leader Lloyd George after the First World War to describe the society he wanted to build once the war was over.

Absolute terms Increases or decreases in cost or standard of living that take no account of factors such as inflation.

Appeasement The Conservative policy of compromising with Hitler in order to avoid war from 1937 to 1939.

Arab-Israeli War Also known as the Yom Kippur War, a war between Arab states, including Egypt and Iraq, and Israel.

Authoritarian A form of government that has strict limits on individual freedom.

Balance of payments The total of trade between one country and the rest of the world.

Balance of payments deficit A situation in which one country imports more than it exports.

Beeching Report A report recommending significant cuts in the scope of the railway network.

Brixton and Toxteth riots The two most dramatic examples of urban unrest during the 1981 riots. They were a response to long-term deprivation and police harassment.

Bureaucratisation Increasing the scope of the control of officials.

By-election An election that takes place between general elections caused by the death or resignation of an MP.

Closed shop An agreement between unions and employers that the employers will only employ members of the union.

Coal Board An organisation established in 1945 to manage the nationalised coal industry.

COHSE The Confederation of Health Service Employees is a union representing nurses and other workers in the NHS.

Commons majority A situation where the government can control the House of Commons due to the fact that it has the loyalty of more than half of the MPs.

Convertible A currency that can be freely exchanged for other currencies or gold.

Corporatism An economic system that brings together government, unions and employers in an attempt to improve the economy.

Cronyism Giving special favours, such as money, influence, power or good jobs, to friends.

Deflationary policies Economic policies that are designed to combat inflation, usually by cutting government spending.

Dependency culture An economic system which encourages people to claim benefits rather than work.

Deregulating Removing government controls.

Deutschmark The currency of the Federal Republic of Germany until the adoption of the Euro.

Devolution Giving powers from central government to local government. The term is usually associated with the creation of Parliaments in Scotland and Wales.

'Dries' A nickname for right-wing members of the Conservative Party during the 1980s.

Economic rights Rights relating to an individual's standard of living, e.g. the right to work and the right to healthcare.

European Economic Community (EEC) An organisation created in 1957 with the aim of generating closer economic co-operation between European countries.

Euroscepticism Extreme Eurosceptics argue that Britain should withdraw from Europe. More moderate Eurosceptics are unhappy with some aspects of Britain's relationship with Europe.

Exchange Rate Mechanism (ERM) An economic system introduced in 1979 to harmonise the values of European currencies.

Falklands War A military conflict between Britain and Argentina over the control of the Falkland Islands that lasted from April to June 1982.

Federation of British Industry An organisation founded in 1916 representing 124 businesses. In 1965 it merged with other business groups to create the Confederation of British Industry.

First Past the Post An electoral system where the candidate with the most votes wins the seat. Significantly, the winner does not need the majority of votes. Therefore, critics argue that the system is unfair as it leads to election results that do not accurately reflect the proportion of votes cast.

Fiscal policy The aspect of government economic policy that relates to taxation and spending.

Float freely A metaphor that refers to the price of goods or a currency. Goods or currencies are described as 'freely floating' when their value is determined by market forces rather than being fixed by a government.

Free at the point of delivery A product or service (such as NHS healthcare) that is paid for by taxation, but is free at the point of need.

Full employment An economic condition in which there is a very high level of employment. Most economists and politicians do not use the term to describe 100 per cent employment.

Gallup poll An opinion poll.

GDP Gross Domestic Product – the total wealth produced by a country in a given period.

Hung parliament A parliament in which no party has a majority.

Incomes policy A government initiative which is designed to restrain wage increases.

Indirect taxes Usually taxes on products that are paid at the point when a consumer buys goods.

Industrial Charter A statement of Conservative industrial policy published in 1947 accepting the principle of a mixed economy and full employment.

Inflation A rise in the level of prices in an economy.

International Monetary Fund (IMF) An international organisation founded in 1944 which was designed to lend money to countries experiencing economic difficulties.

Interwar depression A period of slow growth or recession lasting from 1918 to 1939.

Keynesianism An approach to economics that argues that governments should play a role in reducing unemployment by borrowing and spending money.

'Lame duck' A nickname for a failing industry.

Lawson Boom The period from 1986 to 1988 during which the British economy grew quickly.

Lib–Lab Pact An arrangement between Callaghan's Labour Government and the Liberal Party. The Liberals agreed to support the Labour Government in crucial votes in the House of Commons in return for influence over aspects of government policy.

'Little Neddies' Regional Development Agencies – government organisations designed to encourage economic growth in Britain's regions.

Mandate Authority to govern.

Marshall Aid A programme of economic aid offered to Europe by the USA shortly after the end of the Second World War.

Minority government A government which has the support of less than half of the MPs in the House of Commons.

Monetarism An economic theory and policy that focuses on controlling inflation by limiting government spending.

Monetary policy The aspect of government economic policy that relates to interest rates.

Nationalisation The process of taking a private business into state ownership.

'New Jerusalem' A phrase used to describe Labour's vision of a new freer, fairer society.

New Right Groups and thinkers associated with radical conservatism that emerged in the 1970s.

NUPE National Union of Public Employees – a trade union representing public sector workers.

One Nation Conservatism A traditional form of Conservatism that stresses the good of the whole nation, including the poor.

Open University Founded in 1965, the Open University was designed to offer degree courses to mature students and students who wanted to study part-time.

Opportunity cost An economic term used to describe the cost of not choosing the second-best option, once the best option has been selected.

'Pay-pause' A government initiative which is designed to restrain increases in wages.

Peg A pegged exchange rate is a currency system where the values of currencies are linked to help countries trade.

Polytechnic colleges University level colleges offering practical qualifications.

Poor law A basic system of support for the poor which existed in England and Wales prior to the modern welfare state.

Post-war settlement The post-war consensus.

Private enterprise Businesses that are owned by an individual, a group of individuals or a group of shareholders. They are often contrasted with nationalised industries which are owned by the state.

Private Member's Bill A Bill introduced to the House of Commons by an individual MP.

Private sector The part of the economy which is not owned or directly controlled by the government.

Privatisation The process of taking a business out of state control and floating it on the stock market.

Productivity The ratio between the amount of resources used to produce a product and the amount of product produced.

Proportional representation A voting system in which the number of seats won by a party is proportionate to the number of votes received.

Public sector workers People who work for state-run services.

Public works schemes Projects run by the government which are usually designed to improve British infrastructure.

Race Today Collective An organisation of black and Asian radicals who helped organise campaigns for black and Asian rights across Britain in the 1970s and 1980s.

Rates The system of taxation that funded local government prior to the poll tax.

Real terms Increases or decreases in funding which take inflation into account.

Reserve currency A currency that is used by many countries in order to facilitate trade.

'Right to buy' A phrase which was used by the Conservatives to describe their policy of selling council houses. The phrase was controversial as opposition politicians argued that the 'right' conflicted with the rights of future tenants to rent housing at a reasonable rate.

'Roll back the state' A slogan used by the Conservatives to describe their policies of privatisation and deregulation.

Secondary action Strike action in one sector of the economy in support of industrial action in another sector.

Secondary picketing Picketing of locations not directly related to the industrial dispute.

'Selsdon Man' A nickname for Edward Heath's free market policies of the early 1970s. The policies were outlined at the Selsdon Park Hotel.

SERPS State Earnings-Related Pension Scheme. A pension scheme introduced by Labour in 1978 which linked the pension rates to the increase in wage rates.

State of emergency A declaration from the government that gives government ministers special powers to deal with a crisis.

Tidal barrage A dam used to generate electricity.

Trades Union Congress A national organisation representing British trades unions.

Tripartite Divided into three parts.

Unilateral nuclear disarmament A willingness to give up all nuclear arms without requiring other countries to do the same.

Universal system of benefits A welfare system that is available to everyone regardless of their income.

Uprated Increased.

Wage inflation A general increase in the level of wages.

Wage restraint A willingness to accept small or no increases in wages.

Welfare safety net A minimum level of benefits provided by the state which is designed to stop people falling into poverty.

'Wets' A nickname for moderate members of the Conservative Party during the 1980s.

White Paper A report that is designed to be the basis of a law.

Answers

Section 1: Labour Governments, 1945–1951

Page 9, Eliminate irrelevance

Eliminate the sentences: This source was written by the historian Kevin Jefferys in 1992 and so will be an accurate description of what happened.

One of the reasons the Government could not afford the NHS was because of the Korean War, which was fought from 1950–1953.

Page 11, Highlighting integration

Sample 1 is of a higher level.

Page 13, Doing reliability well: Suggested answer

Source 1 is unreliable as a description of the impact of the nationalisation of the coal industry because the author is a Conservative MP and therefore he has a political bias. He will not want to praise the decision of the Labour Government to nationalise the coal industry.

Source 2 is reliable as a description of the impact of the nationalisation of the coal industry because the source is written on a subject which the author – a historian – is an expert.

Page 15, Write the question: suggested answer

Do you agree with the view that living standards declined in the period 1945–1951? Explain your answer using Sources 1, 2 and 3 and your own knowledge.

Section 2: Conservative Governments, 1951–1964

Page 23, Explain the difference: Suggested answer

Source 1 states that unemployment was high for the majority of this period. Source 2, on the other hand, states that the Conservative Party has maintained full employment. The difference could be explained by how Source 2 is an extract from the Conservative Party election manifesto for 1959. This was a document designed to encourage people to vote for the Conservative Party, and therefore this document will give a positive account of the Conservative period in government. Source 1 is written by a historian who does not have a vested interest in the events he describes. Therefore, this source will give a more objective account of unemployment rates.

Page 27, Explain the difference: Suggested answer

Source 1 suggests that the National Economic Development Council will have a limited impact as it has responsibility for tasks that only the Government can carry out. In this sense, it suggests that its creation is of limited significance. In contrast, Source 2 states that the National Economic Development Council is an 'important forward step', suggesting that its creation is extremely significant. The difference could be explained by how Source 1 is from a speech by the leader of the Liberal Party, who will want to criticise Conservative policies, while Source 2's author, Macmillan, will want to praise his own policies.

Page 27, Eliminate irrelevance

Eliminate the sentences: This Council was created in 1962, and, together with the National Economic Development Office, was known as 'Neddy'.

The Council was set up to encourage workers and employers to discuss the ways in which they could work together to help the economy to grow.

(from Hans Daalder's book 'Cabinet Reform in Britain', published in 1963)

Page 29, Doing reliability well: Suggested answer

Source 1 is unreliable as evidence of the character of Harold Macmillan because of the political bias of the author. Gaitskell was leader of the Labour Party and would therefore have reason to present Macmillan, the Conservative Prime Minister, in a negative light.

Source 2 is fairly unreliable as evidence of the character of Harold Macmillan because it is a second-hand report. Warnock has not met Macmillan, but is basing her account of Macmillan's character on interviews she has read. The interviews themselves may contain political bias.

Page 29, Write the question: Suggested answer

Study Sources 1, 2 and 3. How far do the sources agree that 'Macmillan was not very impressive as Prime Minister' (Source 2)?

Page 31, Develop the detail: Suggested answer

Although Source 2 argues that the Labour victory in the general election of 1964 was due to 'the collapse of Conservative strength', there is evidence in the sources to challenge this view. Sources 1 and 3 both argue that the result was due to the strengths of the Labour Party rather than the weaknesses of the Conservatives. Source 1 highlights strengths of leadership, stating that 'Wilson's poll ratings remained way ahead of Home's'. Harold Wilson **became leader of the Labour Party in 1963 and** was younger and more dynamic than his Conservative rival, Lord Home. **Further to this, he had received a grammar school education, in contrast to many Conservative politicians, who had been privately educated.** As a result, Wilson appealed to a wide section of British society. In addition, the sources draw attention to the strengths of Labour policy. Source 1 argues that 'Labour's insistent talk of "thirteen wasted years" of Tory Government succeeded in catching a mood for change'. The Labour Party election was effective at exploiting the weaknesses of the Tories. For example, they **drew attention to economic problems, such as the reduction in economic growth and the high unemployment levels, and** suggested that little economic progress had been made under Conservative Government. Source 3 supports the argument that it was Labour policy that attracted voters to the party. Wilson states that 'we are here because millions of our fellow countrymen … look to us to provide a strong Britain, a healthy Britain, and to create and maintain a new and fair order of society'. **Voters had faith in Labour economic policy and believed that Wilson would be able to solve the economic problems and create 'a healthy Britain' because he held an economics degree from Oxford University.** In this way, the Labour victory in the general election of 1964 was partly due to strengths of leadership and policy on the part of the Labour Party.

Section 3: Consensus under pressure: Labour and Conservative Governments, 1964–1979

Page 37, Spot the mistake: Suggested answer

The paragraph does not get into Level 4 for AO1 because the own knowledge it contains is generalised.

Page 37, Spot the inference

British exports have increased, and Britain's balance of payments situation has improved. (S)

The increase in exports has improved Britain's balance of payments situation. (I)

We should feel proud that exports have increased by 9 per cent. (P)

The Labour Party lost the general election in 1970. (X)

The improvement in Britain's economic situation was a recent development. (I)

Page 39, Write the question: Suggested answer

Use Sources 1, 2 and 3 and your own knowledge. Do you agree with the view that the Labour Governments of 1964–1970 were a failure? Explain your answer using Sources 1, 2 and 3 and your own knowledge.

Page 43, Highlighting integration

Sample 1 is of a higher level.

Page 45, Doing reliability well: Suggested answer

Source 1 is unreliable as evidence of the impact of the economic policies of the Labour Governments in the period 1974–1979 because of political bias and vested interest. The Conservative Party manifesto reflects the strong political bias of the Conservative Party, and the party have a vested interest in persuading people to elect them to government in place of the Labour Party.

Page 45, Develop the detail: Suggested answer

One way in which the Labour Government's economic policies were unsuccessful was the handling of relations with the trade unions. Source 2 argues that evidence of failure can be found in the 'prolonged, bitter wars with organised labour'. These disputes **began in 1975 when Prime Minister Harold Wilson introduced a pay freeze for everyone who earned more than £8600 a year, and** continued until the Winter of Discontent in 1979. Source 3 describes Callaghan's handling of this period as 'poor'. The Winter of Discontent followed Callaghan's decision to restrict pay rises to five per cent a year. **During this period, the public sector unions NUPE and COHSE went on strike** for six weeks, disrupting rubbish collection, sewage treatment and the burial of the dead. **Overall, 29,474,000 days were lost through strike action in 1979.** Source 3 refers to the impact of these strikes, accusing the trade unions of '[thwarting] Britain's chances of success'. In this way, the economic policies of the Labour Governments of 1974–1979 were unsuccessful in the sense that they led to prolonged disputes with the unions, which hindered Britain's economic growth.

Section 4: End of Consensus: Thatcher in power 1979–1990

Page 57, Doing reliability well: Suggested answer

Source 1 is unreliable as a description of the impact of Conservative economic policies in the period 1979–1990 because of the vested interest and political bias of the author. Nigel Lawson was the Conservative Chancellor of the Exchequer, and therefore had a vested interest in presenting economic policy (which was his responsibility) as a success. In addition, as a member of the Conservative Government, he will have a clear political bias which would make him very unlikely to criticise Conservative policy.

Page 57, Write the question: Suggested answer

Use Sources 1, 2 and 3 and your own knowledge. Do you agree with the view that Conservative economic policy in the years 1979–1989 was a success? Explain your answer using Sources 1, 2 and 3 and your own knowledge.

Page 59, Spot the mistake: Suggested answer

The paragraph does not get into Level 4 because it does not contain a detailed comparison of similarities and differences between the sources.

Page 59, Spot the inference

The miners were not willing to compromise with the Government. (I)

The Conservative Government was willing to settle the strike on terms that was reasonable. (P)

The Conservative Government was willing to compromise in order to end the strike. (I)

Margaret Thatcher regretted having to order the closure of the mines. (X)

Page 61, Explain the difference: Suggested answer

Source 2 states that the Labour Party supported the introduction of a national curriculum. Source 3, on the other hand, suggests that the Labour Party in Stockton opposed the introduction of the National Curriculum. The difference could be explained by the content and provenance of the sources. Source 2 is referring to the Parliamentary Labour Party – that is, the Labour MPs who sit in Parliament. In contrast, Source 3 describes the opinions of a local branch of the Labour Party. Therefore, the sources are referring to two different groups of people. In addition, Source 3 is from a speech by a Conservative MP, who, for political reasons, may wish to portray the Labour Party as out of touch with the views of the people of Britain. This would explain the reference in the source to the difference between the views of the county and the views of the local Labour Party.

Page 67, Develop the detail: Suggested answer

In addition to the resignation of Geoffrey Howe, divisions over Conservative policies were responsible for the downfall of Margaret Thatcher. First, the introduction of the poll tax **in 1988** was unpopular with both the public and members of the Conservative Government. In Source 3, Geoffrey Howe recalls that 'her commitment to the poll tax was almost certainly taking us to disaster'. **In March 1990, 200,000 people marched against the tax in London, and 50,000 joined protests in Glasgow. Thatcher's refusal to reconsider the tax in the face of such opposition indicated to many in her party that she was out of touch with the electorate.** Her views on Europe also faced opposition within the Conservative Party. Source 1 refers to 'repeated rows over monetary union with Britain's European partners'. In addition, Source 2 states that '[Howe] said that his loyalty to Mrs Thatcher conflicted with what he perceived "to be the best interests of the nation"'. **Howe, along with Nigel Lawson, believed that Britain would benefit from joining the Exchange Rate Mechanism, linking the value of the pound to that of other European countries. They believed that this would end the problem of inflation, and keep Britain competitive internationally.** Thatcher's reluctance to develop a closer relationship with Europe created a divide within her Cabinet. In this way, divisions over the poll tax and Europe isolated Thatcher within her Government.

Mark scheme

For some of the activities in the book it will be useful to refer to the mark scheme.
Below is the mark scheme for Unit 2.

Part (a)

Level	Marks	Description
1	1–5	• Selects relevant material from the sources • No attempt to compare the sources • Sources are copied or paraphrased *Level 1 answers are highly simplistic.*
2	6–10	• Selects relevant material from the sources • Notes similarities and differences between the sources • Simple conclusions about provenance *Level 2 answers have some focus on the question, but significant weaknesses. For example, comparisons may be superficial or the answer may demonstrate some misunderstanding of the sources.*
3	11–15	• Selects relevant information from the sources • Detailed comparison of similarities and differences • Begins to use provenance to explain similarities and differences between accounts • Begins to answer 'how far…?' *Level 3 answers address the question and demonstrate a good understanding of how the sources agree and differ.*
4	16–20	• Selects relevant information from the sources • Detailed comparison of similarities and differences • Provenance is used to explain similarities and differences between accounts and to weigh the evidence • Sustained focus on 'how far…?' *Level 4 answers clearly answer the question and demonstrate a sophisticated understanding of the evidence of the sources in their historical context.*

Part (b)

AO1: Using historical knowledge to form an explanation

Level	Marks	Description
1	1–6	• General points with limited focus on the question • Inaccurate supporting evidence • No integration of sources and own knowledge
2	7–12	• General points with some focus on the question • Accurate and relevant – but generalised – supporting evidence • Attempts integration of sources and own knowledge
3	13–18	• General points with secure focus on the question • Mostly accurate and relevant supporting evidence • Some integration of sources and own knowledge
4	19–24	• General points with strong focus on the question • Accurate and relevant supporting evidence • Integration of sources and own knowledge

AO2: Analysing source material

Level	Marks	Description
1	1–4	• Copied or paraphrased information from the sources • Little focus on the question
2	5–8	• Information from the sources is summarised and used to provide a simple answer to the question
3	9–12	• Evidence from the sources is selected to support and challenge the view expressed in the question
4	13–16	• As Level 3 • Weighs the evidence of the sources and uses this in reaching an overall judgment